THE

TOUR BOOK

THE

MISSOURI
U S
66

TOUR BOOK

CURTIS ENTERPRISES
Lake St. Louis

The Missouri US 66 Tour Book. Copyright © 1994 by C.H. Curtis.

Printed in the United States of America

Library of Congress Catalog Card Number: 94-94615

Production by:
D.I. Enterprises. St. Louis, Missouri

Published by:

CURTIS ENTERPRISES
424 S. National
Springfield, MO 65802
417-866-4743

ISBN 0-9633863-4-4

To Mom and Dad for your love. And for the trips you took us kids up Route 66 to St. Louis to see our Cardinals play at Sportsman's Park.

PREFACE

The most famous road in America was commissioned U.S. Highway 66 on November 11, 1926. Stretching 2400 miles from Chicago, Illinois through eight states to California, "Route 66" meandered over 300 miles in ten counties in Missouri. Roughly following the Kickapoo Trace and stagecoach routes, US 66 in Missouri had been variously called the Old Wire Road, Osage Trail, Ozark Trail, Springfield Road, and MO 14. From St. Louis, the highway traveled west through the Meramec River valley, over flat prairies, through the rugged beauty of the Ozark hills, along the Springfield plateau and Ozark Plains, into the mining districts of the Carthage-Joplin area.

The Missouri US 66 Tour Book is intended to aid you in your trek along "old" 2-lane Route 66 in Missouri, whether "touring" in your home or experiencing the "Show Me State" on the open road. (Construction began on 4-lane "new" 66 in the early 1950s, later becoming Interstate 44.) It contains detailed instructions on how to travel the highway in either direction across the state, including accurate maps, milage **(21m)**, and notations [NOTE] concerning bypassed sections no longer accessible. But, foremost, it is a tour book of pictures: over 350 vintage postcards and photographs **(P21)** of Missouri US 66 (1/3 never-before-published), all with captioned histories, which collectively present a history of the highway.

We hope this tour book will enhance your appreciation of the old road, acquainting (or re-acquainting) you with the people, businesses, sites, and facilities in Missouri that served Route 66 for over fifty years. As you travel the tree-lined, picturesque Missouri US 66, take some extra time, go slow, and give a little wave to the "locals" and the other "roadies."

CONTENTS

THE

MISSOURI
US
66

TOUR BOOK

St. Louis to Joplin

ST. LOUIS. (Pop. 396,685). **A town was laid out in 1762 by Pierre Laclede and dedicated to St. Louis IX, name-saint of Louis XV, then King of France. St. Louis IX was the devout and gallant French king in the 13th century, referred to by historians as the "Crusader King." The "Gateway to the West," St. Louis has been under three flags in its history: Spanish, French and American. Home of the Gateway Arch, St. Louis is the largest city on Route 66 between Chicago and Los Angeles.**

US 66 has traversed St. Louis in a variety of ways. The course changed as the city grew and new bypasses were selected to avoid downtown traffic congestion. Listed are three general routes, all ending in Gray Summit, Missouri: 1) CITY 66 (below); 2) ORIGINAL CITY 66 (page 4); 3) BYPASS 66 (page 6). To best experience the feel of Route 66, it is recommended the motorist use a combination: CITY 66 to Jct. Watson Road & Kirkwood. Right on Kirkwood (BYPASS 66) to Jct. Manchester Road & Kirkwood. Left on Manchester (ORIGINAL CITY 66) to Gray Summit.

1) CITY 66. *(Recommended Route)*

[*NOTE: This became the main route in 1933, although you could also enter St. Louis via Municipal Bridge* (**P1**).]

Enter St. Louis via the McKinley Bridge (**P2**). Take Salisbury 1/2 mile to Natural Bridge Av (Palm-1st stop light). Left 1/2 mile, then right on N. Florissant, through the "S" curves onto Tucker (12th Street). Follow Tucker past the Jefferson Hotel (R)(415 Tucker) (**P3**) to Market Street. Civil Courts building (L) (**P4**). City Hall (R) (**P5**). Continue south on Tucker 1-1/2 miles, past Chouteau Av (Checkerboard Square -

Ralston Purina world headquarters) to Gravois Av (French for "gravel"). Veer right onto Gravois 3 miles, past St. Francis De Sales Church (R) **(P6)**, and Arrow Motors (R)(3185), on the site of Edmond's Restaurant **(P7)**, to the 4000 block. Jct. Chippewa Av. (Algonquian for "puckered," referring to a moccasin style with puckered seams.) Right. Follow Chippewa 3 miles, under the MoPac railroad overpass (1940) with its U-turn ramps above and pedestrian walkway below, past Keller Drugs (R)(5201) (1934), Garavelli's Restaurant (L)(6600), once the Shangri-La **(P8)**, to Ted Drewes Frozen Custard (L)(6726) **(P9)**. Continue over the River Des Peres ("de-pair," from the French for "of the Fathers").

SHREWSBURY. (Pop. 6,416). **Platted in 1889, the town was named for a hamlet in England.**
Chippewa becomes Watson Road. Follow Watson Road under the old wooden Frisco railroad trestle (1931).

MARLBOROUGH. Coral Court (R)(7755) **(P10)** and Wayside Court (L)(7800) **(P11)**. Continue on Watson Road past the Chippewa Motel (L)(7880) **(P12)**, Duplex Motel (L)(7898) **(P13)**, and La Casa Grande Court (L)(8208) (c.1940) "Like A Fine Hotel.". Watson Plaza Auto Court (L)(8730) on the site of what was the 66 Auto Court **(P14)**.

CRESTWOOD (Pop. 11,229). Gundaker Realtors (L)(9282), the site where Motel Royal was located **(P15)**. Across the road, Roosevelt Bank (R)(9285), site of The Oaks Motel **(P16)**. National Food Store center (L), site of the old "66" Park In Theatre. Operating continuously from 1946 to 1994, the theatre once offered such pre-movie extras as free pony rides, a Ferris wheel, slides, merry-go-round, and even a pair of trained bear cubs! Crestwood Medical Office Center (L)(10000), on the site of the Blue Haven Auto Court **(P17)**. Blue Bonnet Court **(P18)**, presently Johnny Mac's Sporting Goods (L)(10100). Twin-Six Auto Court **(P19)** was located on the lot (L)(10230) adjacent to Color Art. Jct US 67 (Kirkwood Rd) cloverleaf **(P20)**.

Jct. Watson Road & US 67 (Kirkwood Rd).

EITHER: Right on Kirkwood Rd (BYPASS 66) *(Recommended Route)*

KIRKWOOD. (Pop. 27,291). **This was the first planned residential community west of the Mississippi River. Originally called Dry Ridge, then Collins Station, in 1852 the newly organized town was renamed for James Pugh Kirkwood, chief engineer of the Pacific Railroad, who had laid out the route to the area being sold by land developers.**
Westward Motel (R) **(P21)**. Follow Kirkwood Rd to Manchester Rd, passing the Magic House (R)(516 Kirkwood), a children's museum housed in a mansion built (1901) by the A.G. Edwards brokerage family, Spencer's Grill (L)(223) **(P22)**, and the Missouri Pacific Depot (L) **(P23)**.

Jct. Manchester Road & Kirkwood Rd. West (left) on Manchester Road toward Gray Summit. (See <u>Original City 66</u> - Jct. Manchester Road & Kirkwood Rd, page 4.)

OR: Continue on City 66 (Watson Road - MO 366) to I-44 West.

<u>City 66</u> - Jct. Watson Road & US 67 (Kirkwood Rd).
Odometer Notation: (0.0m)

Viking Conference Center (R), site of Nelson's Cafe **(P24)** and Holiday Inn (R), where Park Plaza Court **(P25)** once was.

[*NOTE: Route 66 is under I-44 for the next 16 miles, except as noted.*]

Travel I-44 West. Prior to crossing the Meramec River (a tribal word for "catfish"), is the site of the old Sylvan Beach Park (R) **(P26)**.

FENTON. (Pop. 3,346). **A post office since 1833, founder William Lindsay Long named the town for his Welsh grandmother, Elizabeth Fenton Bennett.**
The Rose Lawn Motel (L). Next door, what's left of the Siesta Motel. Maritz Inc building (L), on the site of Dudley's Cabins and Service **(P27)**. The Valley Mount Ranch (L), offering horseback riding since 1936. Area (L) at end of I-44 concrete median that was the site of the old Trav-O-Tel Deluxe Court **(P28)**. Views of 66 **(P29, P30)**.

[*NOTE: At* **(11m)** *Old 66 swung right on Lewis Road, past the old Steiny's Inn (R)* **(P31)***, over the Meramec River bridge (1931) and into Times Beach, then crossed to the left of I-44 to Eureka.*]

Cross the Meramec River again.

(11.5m) TIMES BEACH (R) (Pop. 0). **Times Beach was created to be a summer resort on the Meramec River as a promotional gimmick by the St. Louis *Star-Times* in 1925. The newspaper gave away 6-month subscriptions to all who bought a parcel lot, and held contests to give away other lots. In 1972-73, its dusty streets were sprayed with waste oil. In 1982 the town received global notoriety when the Environmental Protection Agency disclosed that the oil contained dioxin, and that the entire town was contaminated. By 1986 a government buyout was complete, and Times Beach ceased to exist.**

(13m) EUREKA. (Pop. 4,683). **In 1853 a surveying engineer for the railroad discovered that a route through this valley would eliminate many cuts and grades, and called the construction camp "Eureka" (Greek, meaning "I have found it!").**

(15.5m) Allenton/Six Flags Exit 261. Leave I-44 here, left under the interstate to Jct. Business Loop 44.

ALLENTON. Named for Senator Thomas R. Allen, president of the Pacific Railroad Company, who had laid out the town in 1852.
The Henry Shaw Gardenway School Bus Stop (L) (c.1939). Right on Business Loop 44 (US 66), past the Al-Pac **(P32, P33)** and old Beacon Court (R) **(P34)**. Cross bridge (1932) over Fox Creek.

(23m) PACIFIC. (Pop. 4,350). The Pacific Railroad Company laid out the town in 1852 on their way to the Pacific Ocean. Called Franklin, another name had to be taken for the new post office in 1854. The building of the railroad had been stalled here for a couple of years (some money problems), so residents renamed the town for the railroad's hoped-for destination.
Red Cedar Inn (R) **(P35)** and Jensen Point (R) **(P36)**. Continue on Loop 44 past the "caves" (R) **(P37)** and through town. Across from more caves is a used car lot (L) that was the Cave Cafe **(P38)**. **(24m)** The old Trail's End Motel (L) **(P39)**. Bridge (1932) over a deep cut for the Missouri Pacific tracks that tunnel *under* the town of Gray Summit. **(25m)** Jct. MO 100. (See **GRAY SUMMIT**, page 8.)

2) ORIGINAL CITY 66.

[*NOTE: This was the primary route from 1926 to 1932.*]

Enter St. Louis via the McKinley Bridge **(P2)**. Take Salisbury 1/2 mile to Natural Bridge Av (Palm-1st stop light). Left 1/2 mile, then right on N. Florissant, through the "S" curves onto Tucker (12th Street). Follow Tucker 3 miles past the Jefferson Hotel (R)(415) **(P3)** to Market Street **(3m)**. Civil Courts building (L) **(P4)**. City Hall (R) **(P5)**. Right on Market Street (the main road used by fur-trading Indians and farmers bringing their produce to market). Kiel Center (L), originally called Municipal Auditorium **(P40)**. Union Station (L) **(P41)**.

[*NOTE: West of here, Market was cut off (by US 40 - 1937) as it became Manchester Road.*]

Veer right onto Forest Park Pkwy one mile, left on Vandeventer 1/2 mile (2 stop lights) to Manchester Road. Right on Manchester 6 miles through **MAPLEWOOD** (Pop. 9,962) and **BRENTWOOD** (Pop. 8,150) to **ROCK HILL** (Pop. 5,217). Trainwreck Saloon (R)(9243), originally the 9-Mile House **(P42)**. Continue west 3 miles through **GLENDALE** to **KIRKWOOD**. (See page 2 for Kirkwood notes.)

Original City 66 - Jct. Manchester Road & Kirkwood Rd.
Odometer Notation: (0.0m)

West on Manchester, the original route of US 66 (1926-1932)

(1m) DES PERES. (Pop. 8,388). Named for the River Des Peres ("de-pair," from the French for "of the Fathers"). The area has had a post office since 1848.

(2m) Village Bar (R)(12247) next to the Diem House **(P43)**. Continue west over I-270.

(5.5m) MANCHESTER. (Pop. 6,542). **Originally called Hoardstown (after Jesse Hoard), it was changed in 1824 to Manchester by a local landowner from Manchester, England. Others say it was named for a settler who had been in the area as early as 1795, "old Mr. Manchester."**

(6m) Jct. MO 141 (Woods Mill Rd). City Hall is in the Lyceum (L)(14318). Built in 1894, it originally housed a tin shop and mercantile downstairs, and an auditorium upstairs. (On the National Register of Historic Places.) The Springs Bar & Grill (L)(14424), once the Tourist Hotel **(P44)**.

(6.5m) WINCHESTER. (Pop. 2,027). **Incorporated in 1935, the name is a combination of neighboring towns Ballwin and Manchester.**

(7.5m) BALLWIN. (Pop. 21,816). **Named for John Ball, who had platted a town in 1837 on his farm near Fish Pot Creek.**

(9m) ELLISVILLE. (Pop. 6,233). **William Hereford established a post office here in 1843, and probably named it for his hometown in Virginia. Some believe the name honored the man who later developed Ellisville, Vespuccio Ellis, longtime United States Consul to Venezuela.**

(10m) Jct. Clarkson Road.

[*NOTE: Old 66 went under MO 100 for 1-1/2 miles, swung right uphill, then left downhill.*]

Straight on MO 100 1-1/2 miles to Manchester Rd. Left.

[*NOTE: Old 66 rejoins Manchester Rd by the bottom of a hill at* **(12m)**. *(A 1/4-mile stretch is visible to the right, climbing up the hill.)*]

The Calvery Christian Church (R) is the site of "Hill Side View," the roadhouse and grounds that overlooked a curve in Old 66 where the contestants in the 1928 "International-Trans-Continental Foot Race" **(P45)** spent the night.

(13m) GROVER. **Once known as St. Friedling, a post office was awarded the town during the administration of Grover Cleveland, and renamed in honor of him.**
Cross Jct. MO 109.

(14m) POND. Settled in the 1820s, it was first called Speer's Pond, for Cyrus Speer, a local millowner.
Pond Inn "Tavern" (L) **(P46)**. Pond Hotel (L) (c.1840), now a residence. Just west of here is part of the Big Chief Hotel (L) **(P47, P48)**.

(16m) FOX CREEK. A post office from 1833-1904. Although the settlement was located at the headwaters of Wild Horse Creek, it was named for the nearby Fox Creek (which was so-called by a local hunter after he had shot an extremely large fox there). The new MO 100 cut through what was left of the town. Not much remains.

(16.5m) Cross over MO 100. Continue on Manchester 1/2 mile, past the Ace Case building that was once Fox Creek Garage (L) **(P49)**, to Jct. Melrose Road & MO 100.

[*NOTE: Old 66 crossed to the left of MO 100 here, and ran parallel for 2-1/2 miles.*]

Right on MO 100.

(18m) HOLLOW. A relay station for the old St. Louis & Jefferson City Stage Line (now West County Horsemen's Club). For a time, the settlement was known as Dutch Hollow, for "Mine Host Dutch Charles," as Charley Pfaffath, who conducted a popular tavern (L) in this small valley, was familiarly known.

(19.5m) Right on Manchester Road (Old 66). Continue west, over Fox Creek bridge (1923) to Jct. MO 100 & CO. OO **(21.5m)**. Right on MO 100 (Old 66) 7 miles, past Bahr Discount Foods (R), on the site of the old Motor Inn **(P50)**, down Tucker Hill to Gray Summit.

(28.5m) GRAY SUMMIT. At the bottom of Tucker hill (Rd 105 242) is a residence (L) with metal roof and enclosed front porch that was Summit Cottage **(P51)**. Bel-Air Awning (R), once Tucker Hill Transfer (c.1923), owned by Gene and George Smith, who lived in houses on both sides of the business. Jct. CO. MM.

[Leave 66 here one mile to the right to Purina Farms, with domestic animals and activities open to the public since 1925.]

Continue on MO 100 and cross over I-44.
(See **GRAY SUMMIT**, page 8.)

3) BYPASS 66.

Enter St. Louis via the new Chain of Rocks Bridge on I-270.

[*NOTE: This bypass was established in the early 1930s and designated Route 66 in 1936.*]

[Take Riverview Drive south to view the "unique" old Chain of Rocks Bridge (**P52**, **P53**). Close to the Missouri shore is the "Fortress," Intake Tower No. 1 (1894), used to draw water into St. Louis' system (crew quarters are above). Intake Tower No.2 (1915) is closer to the old bridge]
Jct. Riverview Drive & I-270.

[*NOTE: BYPASS 66 is under I-270 (1961) for the next 9 miles to Lindbergh Blvd.*]

West on I-270.

BELLEFONTAINE NEIGHBORS. (Pop. 10,922). Derived from the French "belle fontaine" (beautiful spring). Fort Bellefontaine (1805) was the first fort west of the Mississippi River.

FLORISSANT. (Pop. 51,208). "Missouri French" for "fleurissant," meaning flowering, prosperous, or flourishing.
The John B. Myers House & Barn (R) (**P54**).

HAZELWOOD. (Pop. 15,512). Probably named after Hazelwood Farms. Senator Henry Clay of Kentucky, on a visit here in 1828, proclaimed a local orchard reminded him of his estate "Hazelwood." The owner renamed his farm, and the area followed suit.
Jct. I-270 & Lindbergh Exit 25A. Aerial view of 66 (**P55**). Leave I-270 here on Lindbergh South (US 67), past the Airport Motel (R)(6221 Lindbergh) (**P56**).

BRIDGETON. (Pop. 17,779). Called Cottonwood Swamp, it was renamed Bridgeton in the early 1840s because one had to cross a stone bridge to reach town from either direction.
Site (L) Lambert Air Field (**P57**). Continue over Natural Bridge Road. Stanley Cour-Tel (R)(4675) (**P58**). Cross over I-70. Air-Way Motel (R)(4125), once Air-O-Way Courts (**P59**). Cross over St. Charles Rock Rd (old US 40). Northwest Plaza entrance (L)(3700 block), once the site of the Sunset Acres Motel (**P60**).

MARYLAND HEIGHTS. (Pop. 25,407). A post office since 1925, a local doctor from Maryland named his estate high on a hill "Maryland Heights."

CREVE COEUR. (Pop. 12,304). French for "broken heart," locals say the town received its name from the legend of an Indian maiden who was "heart-broken" because her love, a French trapper, never returned. She is said to have cried tears that formed a lake in the shape of a broken heart, then drowned herself in its waters.
World Headquarters for Monsanto (R-L).

FRONTENAC. (Pop. 3,411). Named to honor the 17th century governor of Quebec, Louis de Baude, Comte De Palluau et De Frontenac (Count Frontenac).
Continue on Lindbergh under new US 40 (I-64). Frontenac Hilton (R)(1335), on the site of the old King Bros. Motel (**P61**).

(23m) Jct. Manchester Road & Kirkwood/Lindbergh.

EITHER: Turn right (west) on Manchester *(Recommended Route)*
(See Original City 66 - Jct. Manchester Road & Kirkwood Rd, bottom of page 4),

OR: Straight, through Kirkwood to Jct. Watson Road (City 66).

KIRKWOOD. (Pop. 27,291). **This was the first planned residential community west of the Mississippi River. Originally called Dry Ridge, then Collins Station, in 1852 the newly organized town was renamed for James Pugh Kirkwood, chief engineer of the Pacific Railroad, who had laid out the route to the area being sold by land developers.**
Missouri Pacific Depot (R) **(P23)**. Spencer's Grill (R)(223) **(P22)**. The Magic House (L)(516), a children's museum housed in a mansion (1901) built by the A.G. Edwards brokerage family. Proceed under I-44, past the Westward Motel (L) **(P21)**. Jct. Watson Road & Kirkwood cloverleaf **(P20)**. Right (west) on Watson Road toward I-44. (See City 66 - Jct. Watson Road & US 67 (Kirkwood Rd), page 3).

GRAY SUMMIT. (Pop. 2,505). **At one time called Point Labadie, it was renamed for Daniel Gray, who kept a hotel here (1841), the highest point on the railroad between St. Louis and Jefferson City.**

Jct. MO 100 & I-44.
Odometer Notation: (0.0m)

West on MO 100 (Old 66). The Missouri Botanical Garden's Shaw Arboretum (L) (1925), 2400 acres of cultivated trees and plants (opened to the public in 1940), designed to preserve for the future a typical example of Ozark landscape. Site (R) of an old Missouri Highway Weight Station **(P62)** by Diamonds Restaurant. El Paso Auction/Trading Post (R), once Cozy Dine Cafe **(P63)**. Gardenway Motel (L) **(P64)**. Brush Creek Cemetery (R) with gravestones dating to the 1820s. Cross over I-44. Wayside Farmers Market (L) and (next door) the old Mingle Inn **(P65)**. **(2m)** Jct. MO 100 & CO. AT. Continue west on CO. AT, past Tri-County Truck Stop (R), originally The Diamonds **(P66)**. **(3m)** Sunset Motel (R) **(P67)**. Child care center (L) that was the old American Inn **(P68)**.
(5m) Jct. CO. M. **VILLA RIDGE.** (Pop. 1,865). **A Mr. Emerson, supervisor of the railroad construction in the 1880s, named the new station for the ridge that forms a watershed between the Meramec and Missouri Rivers; and "villa," Spanish for town.**
Guffey's Store (L), once the office/grocery for Stropman's Camp (c.1928), with cabins on the side and in back. What once was Hobbleburger's Tavern, Cafe/Grocery (R) (c. 1940). Keys Twin Bridge Cafe (L), built in 1945. U-Store-It units (L), once the Pin Oak Motel **(P69)**.

[*NOTE: Old 66 crossed the Bourbeuse River (pronounced "burr-bus," French for "muddy") on the "Twin Bridges"* **(P70)**. *It then crossed the valley to the right of I-44 outer road.*]

Cross over US 50 to CO. AH. West on outer road.

[*NOTE: Old 66 was by the power poles, moved left under I-44, then to the outer road again.*]

(9m) Oak Grove Tavern (R) (1928), a store/tavern with Sinclair pumps in front, and four cabins in back, now expanded into homes. What's left of the 41 Mile Post (L) (1930s), once consisting of a tavern, store, and cabins. The store closed around 1947.

[*NOTE: Old 66 swung left, under I-44 for 1 mile.*]

(10m) HALL'S PLACE. During Prohibition, Frank Hall, a local bootlegger, built his "community" here, a house, Sinclair gas station, and store (R). He also had a "bar & barn" dancehall, and at one time, he boasted, seventeen stills (P71).
Continue west, past the old Four Seasons (1927), once comprised of a gas station, tavern and cabins built by Tom Hoff. It was the first local business on the newly paved US 66. Wind up around the hill.

[*NOTE: Old 66 began to angle down the valley, under the overpass, ending to the left of I-44.*]

(12m) Left over I-44. Right on South Outer Road West, rejoining Old 66.

(14m) ST. CLAIR. (Pop. 3,917). Called Traveler's Repose (after a wayside inn & tavern), the name was changed so others wouldn't think of it as a "pioneer cemetery." It was renamed for a resident civil engineer of the Frisco Railroad in 1859.
Napa Auto Parts (L), once Le Claire Motors **(P72)**. Jct. MO 47. Follow Old 66 (MO 47-Commercial Street) through town, past the old Johnson's Mo-Tel Cabins (Art's) (L) **(P73, P74)**, now occupied by Coldwell Banker Realty, apartments (R) at top of hill, once the Hi Spot Inn **(P75)**, and what was The Chuck Wagon Cafe and St. Clair Chronicle (R) **(P76)**. Continue through the blinking traffic light to Jct. MO 30 **(15.5m)**. On the (L) is what once was Harty's Dine-O-Tel **(P77)**.

[*NOTE: Old 66 is cut off 1-1/2 miles further, past Ritter & Sons Garage **(P79, P80)**, once Shady Shell **(P78)**, and the St. Clair Motel **(P81)**.*]

Right on MO 30, over I-44. Left on CO. WW.

[*NOTE: Old 66 stayed next to the tracks, left of I-44.*]

Agape House (R), once Scully's Sunset Inn **(P82, P83)**. Straight on outer road.

[*NOTE: Old 66 continued next to the railroad (at times under the I-44 eastbound lane), past a residence (L) that was the second location of Ozark Rock Curios* **(P84)**, *crossed to the north outer road by the I-44 "Rest Area Left Lane" sign, wound down "Coal Mine Hill", swung out under the I-44 westbound lane by Rest Area (site of old coal mines), then back right, up the hill.*]

(20.5m) Jct. St. Louis Inn Road. Salvage yard (L), site of what was Leroney's **(P85)**.

[*NOTE: Old 66 swung to the left of Ozark Court (R)* **(P86)**, *past an area (R) that once was The Tepee* **(P87)**, *and past the old Trade Winds Motel, then back to the right outer road.*]

(22m) Remains of Benson's Tourist City (R) **(P88)**.

[*NOTE: Old 66 gradually moved left here, past an empty building at Lollar Branch Rd (R) that once was the Motel Meramec* **(P89)**, *and Happy Acres Home (R), once Shady Rest Court, under I-44 eastbound lane, then next to the tracks into Stanton.*]

(24.5m) Left over I-44.
STANTON. Originally Reedville, the town was renamed for the Stanton Copper Mines, owned by John Stanton (c. 1856).
Jct. South Outer Road West. Aerial view of 66 **(P90)**.

[Leave 66 here, on CO. W, to see Meramec Caverns **(P91)**.]

Right on Old 66 (South Outer Road West). Jesse James Museum (L), in business over 30 years. Antique Toy Museum (L), in an old Stuckey's Restaurant. Stanton Motel (R-across I-44) **(P92)**. Hideout Cavern City Court (Motel) (R) **(P93)**. **OAK GROVE VILLAGE.** (Pop. 421). Cross Winsel Creek bridge (1922). 1/10th mile to some trailers (L), site of the old Martha Jane Farm Auto Court **(P94, P95)**.

Cross Jct. MO 185. **(29.5m) SULLIVAN.** (Pop. 5,661). **In 1859 the town name was changed from Mount Helicon to thank Stephen Sullivan, who had laid out a new town, given land for the Frisco depot, and had even built the station himself.**
Follow Springfield Road (Old 66) through town. At the stop sign, drug store (L) where the White Swan Restaurant **(P96)** once was, St. Anthonys School (R), site of the Sullmo Hotel & Cabins **(P97)**. Chamber of Commerce building (L), once Campbell Chevrolet **(P98)**, and next door an insurance agency that was Juergens Station **(P99)**. "Sunny" Jim Bottomley Park (L), named for the former St. Louis Cardinal baseball player (and Hall of Famer) who set the major league record for most RBI's in a single game-12 (1924). 4-way stop (Elmont Rd). Scott Welding (L) (1940s), once Standard Garage (1927), opened 24 hours a day with four mechanics on duty, and Sull-Mo Music, once Westgate Manor (1926).

[*NOTE: Old 66 is interrupted briefly one block further.*]

Right on Elmont, left on S. Service Rd. past CO. D.

[*NOTE: 66 rejoins outer road here.*]

Shamrock Court (Motel) (L) (**100**). (**36m**) (Allison) Hill (originally Bourbon) Cemetery (R) dating from the 1840s. The old Friesenham Dairy Farm (R) (**P101**).

(**36.5m**) **BOURBON. In the early 1850s, newly imported bourbon whisky was sold by Richard Turner at his store to railroad construction crews. The business became known as the "Bourbon Store," and eventually the new town was called Bourbon.**
Cross Jct. CO. J & CO. N. Follow the "Old Highway 66" signs (L) around town, past what once was the Roedemeier Garage (R) (**P102**) and the "Bourbon Tower" (R) (**P103**). At the stop sign, Peoples Bank (L), the site of Tiners Place (**P104**). Straight. Drive (R) marked by sign "066-550," the old Marge & Bernie Station (**P105, P106**). 1/10th mile to what was Bourbon Lodge (L) (**P107**). 1/2 mile to the old Hi Hill Station (L) (**P108**). Bridge over Shallow Creek (1924). Jct. CO. H.
[Leave 66 to the left here, through **LEASBURG**, to go to Onondaga Cave (**P109**).]

(**45m**) Railroad crossover (L) marked HR3-000. **HOFFLIN. Named for local landowner William Hofflin. A post office from 1903 to 1943, all that remains are the foundations of the general store and gas pumps (P110).**

(**47m**) **CUBA.** (Pop. 2,537). **In 1857, two gold miners returned home from California via Cuba and expounded on the island's virtues. Impressed, the townspeople called their new post office "Cuba."**

[*NOTE: This section of Route 66 was one-way eastbound from 1953-1968 (New 66). The westbound lanes were part of what is now I-44.*]

On the (R)(1000 block), Cuba Self-Storage, site of the Lazy Y Camp (**P111**). Across from the water tower is the Paul's Cafe building (R) (**P112**). On the (L) is what used to be the Red Horse Cabins (**P113**). Across the road is an example of a "Classic 66" court: the Wagon Wheel Motel (**P114**). Continue into town, past the Hotel Cuba (L)(500 block) (**P115**) and the Cuba Dairy Creme (L)(402) that opened in 1952 as a Dairy Queen; renamed in 1970 by then-owner Fritz Sthrothamp. Jct. Franklin Blvd (MO 19). The old Midway (R) (**P116**). Across the way on the (L) is an old Phillips 66 station (1930s), once operated by the father of Don Carter, the famous St. Louis bowler and member of the Bowling Hall of Fame; later (1940s), Carr's Standard Service and Pontiac Dealership. Peoples Bank (L), site of Barnett Motor Co. (**P117**). Old 66 Cafe (L) (early 1950s). At stop light, title company and law firm (L) that was the Peoples Bank (**P118**). The old B&M Cafe (L)(700W) (**P119**). Route 66 Lounge (R), once the West End Tavern (1951). (This has been the site of a tavern since the 1920s.) Straight on CO. ZZ.

(52.5m) FANNING. Named for the four Fanning brothers, who had worked across Missouri on the railroad construction crews before settling here in 1887.

(56.5m) ROSATI. Settled in 1890 and known as Knobview, in 1930 the local Italian wine growers changed the name to honor Bishop Joseph Rosati, the first Italian bishop of St. Louis. For years there have been many grape stands along Old 66 **(P120)**. Straight on CO. KK.

(60m) ST. JAMES. (Pop. 3,328). The first settlement was called Big Prairie. In 1860 the name was changed to honor Thomas James, who owned the nearby Maramec Iron Works. It was considered more modest to name a town after one's name-saint - in this case, St. James the Apostle.
Jct. Springfield Rd (L)(600 block). Building (L) that was the St. James Inn **(P121)**. Follow James street through town. Jct. Mueller St. (400 block). Building (R) by propane tanks is all that remains of the Atlasta Service Station **(P122)**. Jackson Automotive Service (L)(320) that once was a Delano Oil Co. service station **(P123)**. St. James Auto Repair (R)(103) that was the first of the Delano Oil Co. stations (1930). Jct. MO 68. On the left corner is Johnnie's Bar, originally Rose Cafe **(P124)**.

[*NOTE: Old 66 went straight here along the divided tree-lined James Blvd. (a public improvement project undertaken when US 66 was routed through town) for 1 mile, but is now cut off.*]

Right on MO 68, past the Missouri Veterans Home (R) (1896). Cross I-44. Left on Outer Road West.

[*NOTE: Old 66 crosses I-44 to the outer road at* **(63.5m)**.]

Residence (R) that was Rock Haven Restaurant & Cabins **(P125, P126)**. Country Aire (R), once Dillon Court **(P127)**. Route 66 Motors, originally Delano Thrifty Service and Thrifty Inn restaurant **(P128)**.

[*NOTE: Old 66 went under I-44 prior to Exit 189, and continued for 4 miles.*]

Jct. CO. V. Straight on north outer road (RD 2020). Mule Trading Post (L) (1958 - started in Pacific in 1948).

[*NOTE: Old 66 (RD 2000) joins RD 2020 from the left at Yield sign* **(70.5m)**.]

NORTHWYE. (Pop. 135). Named for the "Y" created by the junction of US 63 and Route 66, north of Rolla. Union hall (L), built on the site of Ramey's Cafe **(P129)**. Jct. US 63.

(71.5m) ROLLA. (Pop. 14,090). When this Pacific Railroad construction town was named in 1858, it is widely believed that locals, many from North Carolina, accepted the suggestion of George Coppedge to name it after Raleigh, his hometown. It was spelled as he pronounced it, "Rolla."

Left on US 63 (Old 66) to Jct. I-44. Drury Inn (L) is the site of the Sinclair Pennant Hotel (**P130**). Cross over I-44. Jct. Cedar Rd. View of 66 (**P131**). The Shell station (L) was the site of the Pennant Tavern (**P132**) & Cafe (**P133**). Lee's Fried Chicken (L), the site of the Colonial Village Hotel (**P134**); Amoco station (R), site of the old Trav-L-Odge (**P135**). Aerial view of 66 (**P136**). Budget Apartments and Denny's (R), once Schuman's Tourist City (**P137**). View of 66 (**P138**). Jct. Pine Street (**72m**).

EITHER: Straight on Bishop (Business Loop 44-Original 66) around town, past the Dairy Queen and Hardee's restaurants (R)(1300 block), site of the old Phelps Modern Cottages (**P139**), to Kingshighway (Original 66), then right one mile to Martin Spring Drive (I-44 south outer road),

OR: Left on Pine (City 66), past the campus of the University of Missouri-Rolla (R) (1871). The Western Historical Manuscript Collection has an office on campus that maintains Route 66 memorabilia and papers that is open to the public (located in room G-3 of the Curtis Law Wilson Library).

[*NOTE: Originally, Pine was City 66 from 12th to 6th both ways, but is now northbound only.*]

Right on 12th, left on Rolla to 6th. On Pine (L), the Uptown Theatre (1940), library - once the old Post Office (**P140**), Boatmen's Bank building that was the Rollamo Theatre (**P141**) (8th Street) and Phelps County Bank building, originally the Hotel Edwin Long (**P142**). On Rolla, the Ritz Theatre (R) (1940). Right on 6th, angle left into Kingshighway to Jct. Bishop Ave (Business Loop 44-City 66). Straight one mile to Martin Spring Drive (I-44 south outer road).

Jct. Business Loop 44 & I-44.
Odometer Notation: (0.0m)

Left on Martin Spring Drive, past the newest location of the Totem Pole Trading Post (L) (1978), and past the water slide (L), site of an old tourist court from the 1930s, operated by Walt Levine. The office is still standing.

(2m) MARTIN SPRING. Prior to Route 66, the nearby springs watered horses and livestock. The area became known as Martin Spring after William Martin opened a store and operated the springhouse (P143).
Rebuilt residence (L) that was Hillside Tavern (late 1920s), once with gas pumps in front and cabins in back. A popular Route 66 tavern/nightclub from the 1930s to 1955, when fire damaged the upper floor. Beaver Creek bridge (1922), now considered to be a one-lane bridge! Home (R) that was Aaron's Old Homestead (R) (**P144**) and log cabin (R). Aaron's Radiator Service (L) (**P145**).

[*NOTE: Old 66 cut straight across to the north of I-44 at* (**4m**), *behind Gauntlet Paint, once the "new" Totem Pole* (**P146**), *and crosses back one mile further, between Lou Hargis' old skating rink (L), part of his tourist camp (1944), and Ramsey's Garage and Cabins (L) (c.1941).*]

(**5.5m**) **DOOLITTLE.** (Pop. 599). **The area called Centerville (halfway between Newburg and Rolla) was renamed and dedicated in 1946 to honor Gen. Jimmy Doolittle, W.W. II flying hero (and Medal of Honor winner), who flew his own bomber to the ceremonies.**
Jct. CO. T, **NEWBURG** turnoff. Malone's Service Station (R) (**P147**). The original Bennett's Catfish & Cabins (R) (**P148, P149**). (**7m**) Log home (R), site of Towell's Store (**P150**). Luther Mathis' Garage (L) (early 1900s). I-44 Antique Mall (R), the old T&T Cafe (**P151**). (**9m**) Jct. I-44.

[*NOTE: Old 66 (Outer Road West - Arlington Outer Rd) is cut off 1-1/2 miles further.*]

Take I-44 West for 4 miles. On New 66 access road (R) (I-44 north outer road), Vernelle's Motel & Restaurant (**P152**), and John's Modern Cabins (c.1935), once consisting of six cabins, a filling station, cafe/novelty shop, and washroom. They were moved to the right to accommodate the widening of Route 66. (**10.5m**) Aerial view of 66 (**P153**). Log home (L), once the gas station of the original Totem Pole Tourist Camp (**P154**) and Trading Post (**P155**).

[*NOTE: Old 66 cut between I-44 lanes here, to the Beacon Hill Motel* (**P156**), *then crossed back to the left of I-44, down and back around to Arlington.*]

ARLINGTON. Laid out by P.C. Harrison and probably named for his hometown in Virginia. Some suggest Arlington was a "corruption" of Arlie, wife of the first storekeeper. The town predates Route 66 and served railroad travelers and vacationers. Due to county lines being redrawn through the years, Arlington has successively been in St. Louis, Gasconade, Crawford, Pulaski, and Phelps counties.

[*NOTE: Old 66 then crossed over the Little Piney River, past* **JEROME,** *to the bluff road. (The Little and Big Piney Rivers owe their name origins to the pine forests along their banks that provided the first important commercial timber in the state.) The road then passed through Stonydell* (**P157**).]

Cross over the New 66 bridge (westbound-1952/eastbound-1966) to Jerome Exit 172 (**13m**). Left on Outer Road West. View of 66 (**P158**). Cluster of trailers around a concrete slab (R) was the site of Pecan Joe's (**P159**). (**15.5m**) Circle dirt drive (R), marking the site of **POWELLVILLE** (**P160, P161**). Onyx Mountain Caverns (R), used for centuries by Native Americans, and advertising "The Largest Indian Shelter Room in Missouri."

(16m) CLEMENTINE. Also known as "Basket Ridge," it became a popular tourist stop along Route 66 for the many stands selling homemade Ozark baskets and novelties, many strung on wires paralleling the highway. A post office was started here in 1891.

Remains of Fisher's Filling Station (L) (c.1935), once with several cabins in back, prior to Route 66 relocation (1952).

[*NOTE: Old 66 angled across I-44 by the stone building that was Bennett's Catfish Cafe* (**P162**).]

(17m) Left on CO. J, over I-44 to CO. Z. Right on CO. Z (Clementine Outer Rd).

[*NOTE: CO. Z, the 4-lane blacktopped New 66 (completely paved in 1945) was built during W.W. II to facilitate traffic to Fort Leonard Wood. This was the first-used and last-replaced (1981) 4-lane section of Route 66 in Missouri.*]

(18m) SPRINGVALE (R). Named for its topographical characteristics, this area had some homes/cabins, along with a service station, cafe, and saloon.

Across from the entry into Hooker, buildings and residence (L) that were the Hillbilly Store (**P163**).

(19m) HOOKER (R). A post office from 1900 to 1955, the town was originally called Pine Bluff. It was later named Hooker (for a local landowning family), as was Hooker Hollow and Hooker Ford. At one time Hooker had a concert band, and, as the *St. Louis Post-Dispatch* reported in 1929, "Missouri's Smallest High School."

[*NOTE: Old 66 (now dirt) went through Hooker (following the power poles), past the Hooker church and cemetery* (**P164**), *swung to the right past Fancher Store* (**P165**), *circled the hill (is now cut off by I-44) and back around to cross 4-lane New 66 (CO. Z).*]

Continue on CO. Z, through the famous Hooker Cut (**P166, P167, P168**) to Jct. Old 66 (2-lane) (**P169**).

[*NOTE: 4-lane New 66 (CO. Z) goes straight, over the Big Piney River bridge (1942), to Jct. Old 66 (2-lane) at the Grand View Market (R), bypassing Devils Elbow.*]

Left onto Old 66. Roubidoux Woodworkers (R), once Dale's Sporting Goods (**P170**). What was Heatherington's Cabins (L) (now a remodeled home). The old Munger-Moss Sandwich Shop (Barbeque) (R) (**P171, P172**), later Elbow Inn (**P173**). Steel thru-truss bridge (1923) over the Big Piney River. Spectacular bluffs! (Listed by the State Planning Commission as one of the seven beauty spots in Missouri.)

(21m) DEVILS ELBOW. The name was given to a severe point on the Big Piney River by lumberjacks trying to float hand-hewn railroad ties downriver to the town of Jerome. They feared and cursed the bend in the river (caused by a large boulder locals say was put there by the devil) that resulted in inevitable log jams, saying it was a "devil of an elbow!"

Site (L) of the old Devils Elbow Cafe (**P174, P175**). Allman's Market (L), once Miller's (**P176**). Next door, the old McCoy's Store & Camp (**P177**). Continue on up the hill. Stone house (L) fronting River Park, once Graham's Resort (**P178**). Scenic overlook (L). View of 66 (**P179**). Grandview Court (R), once Clinton Cabins then Easy Inn (1932). (**22m**) Jct. CO. Z (4-lane New 66).

[*NOTE: Old 66 went straight, past the Grand View Market and Devils Elbow Motel (R)* (**P180**), *across I-44 to the right, through what once was* **MORGAN HEIGHTS**. *(In 1935 there were six cabins here renting for $1 -$1.50 a night.) "Unused" section of original 66* (**P181**). *Old 66 then crossed back to the left of I-44 at Jct. MO 28 & CO. Z.*]

Left on CO. Z. (**23m**) Jct. MO 28 & CO. Z (Old 66). Continue straight on CO. Z. Rental units (R) that were Tower Court (1940s).

(**25m**) **ST. ROBERT.** (Pop. 1,730). **Rev. Robert J. Arnold established a Catholic church outside Fort Wood in an area that had previously been known as Gospel Ridge. The church, and later the town that developed (1951), were named for his patron saint: St. Robert Bellarmine.**
Jct. Missouri Ave (CO. Y - entrance to Fort Wood). Ramada Inn parking lot (R), site of the old Scott Garage (**P182**). Follow Business Loop 44 (4-lane New 66) past the George M. Reed Roadside Park (L) (dedicated1955), the Ranch Motel (L) (**P183**), the Phillips Oakwood Quick Shop (R), once Oakwood Village (**P184**), and cross over I-44.

(**28.5m**) **WAYNESVILLE.** (Pop. 3,207). **In 1834 the new post office was named for Gen. "Mad Anthony" Wayne, hero of the Battle of Stony Point during the American Revolution. He is reported to have told Gen. George Washington, "I'll storm Hell if you'll plan it!" The town was the chief recreational center for Fort Wood personnel during the war.**
On the Square, the Old Stagecoach Stop (R), built in pioneer days, and the Pulaski County Courthouse (R) (**P185**), both on the National Register of Historic Places. Victory Tavern/Waynesville Cafe (L) (**P186**). Cross the Roubidoux Creek bridge (1923) (pronounced "rue-bee-due," and named for an early French fur trader). Funeral home (R) that was Bell Hotel Resort (R) (**P187**). Ed Wilson Garage (L), once Bohannon Cafe & Garage (1934).

[*NOTE: Old 66 crossed to the left of I-44 by Hilltop Motors* (**33.5m**) *and past the S&G Motel.*]

Cross I-44, then right on MO 17.

(**35m**) **BUCKHORN. Originally called Pleasant Grove, it was renamed for the Buckhorn Tavern where stagecoaches stopped on the road from St. Louis to Springfield. (There was a sign over the door with a large pair of antlers.)**
On the (L), church that was the Pleasant Grove Christian Church, built in 1926 and serving continuously as a church since. Directly across the road, Crafts & Gifts store (R) that once was D&D Cafe & Market (**P188, P189**). The old Pleasant Grove Cabins &

Cafe (L) (**P190**). (**36m**) Site (R) of the Normandy (**P191**). Across the road, Vern Smith's old Hillcrest Groceries & Station (L) (**P192**). Jct. CO.P.

LAQUEY. "Lake way" was named for Joseph J. Laquey, who had used his influence to get a post office established (1898) in Parsons Store (Laquey Market).

[*NOTE: The original blacktopped route went right on CO. P 3 miles, through town, left on CO. AA, joining CO. AB. The "new" paved version of 66 went straight.*]

Straight on MO 17, 2-1/2 miles past Jct. CO. AB & CO. AA. Route 66 Flea Market (R). (**41m**) The old Spring Valley Court (L) (1929). Small building in front was the "shower room," and the remodeled house: the store & cafe. Travelers would stop and water their stock (later, cars) from the spring below. (**43m**) Jct. AB 350 (R).

DADTOWN. "Dad" & Betty Lewis built a general store and grist mill here in the early 1900s, and the "town" was named to honor him. His son Marion set up a large tent nearby, featuring the first silent movies the area had seen.
Empty buildings (R) that were the Central Motel & Station (**P193**).

(**44.5m**) **GASCOZARK.** The name is a combination of the Gasconade River and Ozark Mountains. (The French in St. Louis conferred the name Gasconade on an area inhabited by "boastful" settlers who reminded them of a similar group of braggarts from Gascony, back in France. Ozark is a simplified spelling of the French "Aux Arc." Aux is pronounced "oh," meaning "to," and "arc" is short for the Arkansas Indian tribe. Ozark: "to the Arkansas").
Gascozark Trading Post (L), that was Caldwell's Cafe & Court (**P194, P195, P196**) Across the road (R) is the old Gascozark Cafe (**P197, P198**). 1/2 mile further, the Wayside Inn (L), built to be Hancock's Motel (c.1945).

(**45.5m**) **HAZELGREEN.** A post office from 1858 to 1958, Hazelgreen got its name from the many local hazel nut bushes. The town used to have lodges, stores, many homes, and a school. By 1955, 4-lane New 66 had been built through town.
Hazelgreen Cemetery (L) (1840s). Cleared site (L) of what once was Walker Bros. Resort (**P199, P200**). Across the road was the Parsons Lodge (**P201**). Continue straight.

[*NOTE: Prior to 1922, the Gasconade River was crossed at Beck Ford (under what is now I-44), accounting for the sharp angle to the left in the present "new" road.*]

Cross steel thru-truss bridge (1922) over the Gasconade River.

[*NOTE: The twin New 66 bridges were built in 1956.*]

Remains of Eden Resort (L) (**P202**).

[*NOTE: Old 66 crossed to the right of I-44 here, followed the power poles past a group of remodeled buildings that was Sunrise View Tourist Court* **(P203)**, *then back to the left just past Jct. CO. N* **(49.5m)**.]

(50.5m) Jct. CO. T. On the far right corner is a stone building that was part of The Harbor Cafe & Cabins **(P204, P205)**, later Geno's **(P206)**. Straight 2 miles to a trailer (L) that's next to the site of what was Riley's Snack Bar **(P207, P208)**.

(54.5m) Remains of the slab bridge (R) (road X44-331) on the old road to the town of **SLEEPER. Named for the Frisco construction gang foreman James Sleeper, who had run a rail spur to a coal shute where the town was later built (1883).**

(56.5m) Jct. CO. F.

[*NOTE: Old 66 is cut off 1/4 mile west of here.*]

Right on CO. F, over I-44. Left on North Outer Road.

[*NOTE: 66 crosses to the right of I-44 at* **(58m)**.]

Remains of Satellite Cafe & Phillips 66 station (R) **(P209)**. Village Oaks (R), once 4-Acre Court **(P210)**. El Rancho mobile home park (R) that was Vesta Court **(P211, P212)**. Hall-Moore Stuff Co. (R) in an old dairy farm barn built of native stone (1928). Prior to jog in road (due to relocation of 66) is Cromer's Motors (R), on the site of Scotty's Tourist City **(P213)**.

(61.5m) LEBANON. (Pop. 9,983). **Created in 1849 to be the county seat of Laclede County, it was named for Lebanon, Tennessee, from which many of the settlers had come. Harold Bell Wright, author of *The Shepherd of the Hills*, and pastor of the First Christian Church here, began his literary career in Lebanon.**
Follow Seminole/Old Highway 66 into town. Munger Moss Motel (Motor Court) (L) & Restaurant **(P214, P215)**. Remains of Clarks Rock Court (L) **(P216, P217)**. Wrink's Market (R) (1950), originally built to be a 2-story hotel, but never completed. Turn right at stop sign onto Mill Creek Rd. Veer left onto Elm. The old Lenz HoMotel (R) **(P218)**. Next door, what was Camp Joy (R) **(P219, P220)**, and Drake Automotive (R), on the site of Andy's Street Car Diner **(P221, P222)**. Orchard Farms liquor store (R) that was originally a Barnsdall station **(P223)**. Jct. MO 5. On the (R), the Metro office building, once the Union Bus Depot **(P224, P225)**.

[Leave US 66 here to the right 1-1/2 blocks to a Kentucky Fried Chicken restaurant with an extensive Route 66 photo display, and, next door, Lebanon Yamaha, once Montgomery Motor Sales **(P226)**.]

Consumer's Market (L), site of what once was Nelson's Tavern **(P227)**. Country Kitchen (R), site of Nelson's Dream Village **(P228)**. View of 66 **(P229)**. Continue straight on Elm (US 66). Colt Market (R), once a Mobilgas station **(P230)**. **(65.5m)** Jct. CO. W. Turn right on CO. W, then left. B&D Truck Port sign ("Self Service Entrance") from Vesta Court. **(67m)** Slab bridge over Goodwin Branch (1922). **(68.5m)** Tan-colored residence (L), closest to road, once a cabin that has now been moved 1/10th mile from the site of the Bungalow Inn (L) **(P231)**, across from county road X44-716.

[*NOTE: Old 66 crossed to the left of I-44 at* **(69.5m)** *for the next 2 miles.*]

(70m) CAFFEYVILLE. Named for J. Floyd Caffey, local businessman (P232). The 4-lane New 66 razed most of the town.
Old 66 ran in front of the stone Liberty Freewill Baptist Church on the left of I-44 (1950s - on this site since 1907).

[*NOTE: Old 66 crosses back to the right at* **(71m)**.]

Example of barn advertising (R) by Meramec Caverns **(P233)**. Frisco Railroad underpass (1926), referred to as the "subway" when it was built. Many a car transport truck had to let air out of their tires to pass under. Building (R) that was the Underpass Cafe & Station **(P234, P235)**. **(75m)** Jct. CO. C.

[*NOTE: Old 66 crossed to the left of I-44 1/2 mile further, past the Skelly station and the Midway Motel (R)* **(P236)**.]

Cross over I-44.

(75.5m) PHILLIPSBURG. (Pop. 170). Named for Rufus Phillips, who built a store here prior to the Civil War.
Right on CO. CC, past the Phillipsburg school & gymnasium (1937-burned in 1985).

[*NOTE: Rejoin Old 66 at* **(76.5m)**.]

(80m) CONWAY. (Pop. 629). Named for a J. Conway, who was responsible for getting the railroad here in 1869.
Jct. CO. J. Empty corner lot (R) that was the site of Harris Standard Station **(P237)** and Harris Cafe **(P238, P239)**. Continue straight.

(85.5m) Jct. CO. HH. **SAMPSON (L).** **At one point there was a store/post office (1904-1935) and gas station among a few cabins.**
On the far side of the Frisco tracks is part of an old tomato canning factory, one of 17 along the railroad between Marshfield and Cuba operated by Case Canning Co. of Marshfield. In the early 1930s, there were over 300 tomato canning factories here in Webster County alone! The old Timber Hill Camp (R) (c.1935), once three cottages with private cooking facilities, community toilets and showers, renting for $1 - $1.50 (The residence in front was the office.) Abbylee Modern Court (L) **(P240).** Jct. CO. M.

(88.5m) NIANGUA. (Pop. 459). **The town was named after the Niangua River, which was probably so-called for the Indian phrase "ne anoga," which translates "water that runs over a man." Locals say Niangua comes from another phrase meaning "I won't go away," or "I won't go farther," suggesting that this was the site where one would settle.**
Niangua Junction Station/Grocery (R) (c.1935-remodeled 1992). 1 mile further, home (L) that once was Rockhaven Roadhouse & Cabins (c.1925), the area's "most popular night spot for beer and dancing" in the 1930s and '40s. House with cabins (L), once Oak Vale Park (1939-1952), before that Carpenter's Camp, with cafe/service station and outdoor facilities for cooking and picnics (now being restored by owner Alf Smith). **(91m)** Old Phillips 66 station (L) (c.1925), and pony truss bridge (1924) over the Niangua River.

(93m) MARSHFIELD. (Pop. 4,374). **The seat of Webster County, the site was surveyed in 1855 and named for Daniel Webster's Massachusetts home, Marshfield. According to the 1941 edition of the W.P.A.'s *Missouri*, since the tornadoes of 1878/1880 (which killed over 80 townspeople) "things have gone fairly quietly, with only the rise and fall of farm prices to affect the town's tranquility."**
Main Course Cafe (L), once Skyline Cafe **(P241)** by the golf course. As you enter Marshfield, Old 66 is called Hubble Drive, honoring local son Edwin Hubble, the first astronomer to prove the existence of other galaxies, and for whom the Hubble telescope (launched into orbit, 1990) is named. Jct. MO 38. On the (L), Country Express station/store, once Sinclair Tourist Camp **(P242).** Right on Washington (MO 38-Old 66) two blocks, past the Conoco station (R) that was Davison Camp **(P243),** and Tony's Fastop (R), once William's Service Station **(P244),** to Jct. CO. OO (Strafford Road). Left, then right. On the (L), across from Singer Auto Parts, was 66 Motor Court **(P245).** In a few miles there is a lovely one-mile winding climb, past Jct. CO. B (**NORTHVIEW** turnoff) to the site of the old Red Top Court (L) **(P246)** and Otto's Steak House (R) **(P247).**

(104m) HOLMAN. **The Holman family owned land here, creating a store and post office in 1903. Behind the low cobblestone wall (L), Holman Woods consisted of cabins and the Ranch Hotel & Restaurant (P248).**

(107m) STRAFFORD. (Pop. 1,166). With the coming of the railroad in 1870, a town was platted on land that had been a Kickapoo Indian reservation, and named for J. Strafford, a local landowner from Strafford, Connecticut. Strafford was listed in *Ripley's Believe It Or Not* as the only American town with 2 "main streets" and no back alleys. (MO 14, one block to the right, was the main road in town until Route 66 was built between the railroad and the backs of the businesses, which were then extended to meet the new road.)

Merge with MO 125. The A-1 Garage (R), once McDowell Garage **(P249)**. Wee World Daycare (R), once Alexander's Drug Store **(P250)**. **(109m)** MO 125 turns left.

[*NOTE: MO 125 (once MO 14) was the original Route 66 until CO. OO/MO 744 was constructed. To follow, turn left to CO. YY (Division Street), right; continue over US 65, past the Springfield Downtown Airport (L)(2200-2300 block)* **(P251)**, *to Glenstone Ave (City 66). See* <u>City 66</u> *- Jct. Glenstone & Division (page 22).*]

Continue straight on CO. OO. Jct. FR (Farm Road) 209.

(110.5m) NOGO. A junction on the Frisco Railroad into the 1940s, Nogo had a post office from 1896 to 1907. When locals gathered to name the "town" (two stores and a blacksmith shop), there wasn't agreement on any one name. Someone opined that the meeting was a "no-go," a popular phrase of the day. Nogo was then selected.

Dutch's Tavern (R). Follow CO. OO to MO 744 to Springfield.

(112.5m) SPRINGFIELD. (Pop. 140,494). The "Queen City of the Ozarks," and the "Birthplace of Route 66," Springfield was originally a settlement called Campbell and Fulbright Springs. It is generally accepted that during an election to name the new town in 1833, James Wilson (for whom Wilson's Creek, the site of a great Civil War battle, was named) offered a "pull" from his freshly-made white whisky to any who would vote for his choice: Springfield (after the beautiful little town in Massachusetts where he was born).

Springfield was the home of Campbell's 66 Express **(P252)**. **(113m)** The old SoMo Center (L), now Stiles Roofing, on the site of Doc's Place **(P253)**. Bell Motel (L), originally Otto's **(P254, P255)**. Across the road, apartments that were previously Victory Court **(P256)**, Ted's Motor Court **(P257)**, and Red Rooster Motel **(P258)**. Cross over US 65 on Kearney. Remains of Lurvey's Court (R)(2900 Kearney), built by Bert Lurvey in the 1930s, rocked after W.W. II. The reopened Holiday Drive-In (R). East end of Lurvey's Plaza parking lot (R)(2300 block) was Rock View Court **(P259)**. Jct. Barnes Ave. Furniture Factory Outlet (R)(2209) site of the Deluxe Courts **(P260)**. Across the street, in a now empty field, was the Eagle Tourist Court **(P261)**. Rest Haven Motel (L)(2000) **(P262, P263, P264)**. Wal-Mart (R), site of the old Cortez Courts **(P265)**. K Mart (L), site of the Springfield Motor Court **(P266)**. Views of 66 **(P267, P268)**.

(116.5m) Jct. Business Loop 44 (Glenstone Ave) & Kearney (MO 744). There are two basic US 66 routes through Springfield (and an alternate route through "North Springfield"): 1) <u>CITY 66</u> (page 22); 2) <u>BYPASS 66</u> (page 23).

1) <u>CITY 66</u>. *(Recommended Route)*

[Prior to following <u>CITY 66</u>, go straight on MO 744 one block to see an example of a classic Route 66 motel: Rancho Court (L), once Trail's End Motel **(P269)**.]

South on Glenstone 1/2 mile to Jct. Commercial St, passing the Best Inns (R), once Rock Village Court **(P270)**, Maple Motel (R)(2233) **(P271)**, McDonald's (L)(2220), on the site of the South Winds Motel **(P272)**, Ozark Motel (R)(2137), previously New Haven Courts **(P273)**, Skyline Motel (L)(2120) **(P274)**, and Glenstone Cottage Court (R)(2023) **(P275)**. Jct. Commercial St. On the (L), a Brown Derby/Bass Pro Shop on the site of the old Big Boy's Auto Court **(P276)**. Pizza Hut (R), on the site of the Sixty-Six Motor Court **(P277)**, later Heart of the Ozarks Motel **(P278)**.

[*NOTE: To take* **Alternate 66** *(1931), turn right on Commercial 1-1/2 miles to "North Springfield" and its historic, albeit deteriorating architecture. This entire district is listed on the National Register of Historic Places. The town, incorporated in 1871, had as its first "mayor" James J. Barnard, then consolidated with Springfield in 1887. The Frisco Railroad Museum (R) in the old Dispatcher's Building (1943), the only such facility devoted exclusively to the St. Louis-San Francisco Railway. Missouri Hotel (L), previously the Milner Hotel* **(P279)**. *Jefferson Avenue Footbridge spanning the Frisco tracks (R) (1902). Left on Booneville. World Headquarters of the Assemblies of God (R) (in Springfield since 1918), built on the site of White City Park Stadium* **(P280)**. *Greene County Courthouse (L)* **(P281)**, *and across the street (R), Hamby's Steak House* **(P282)**. *Continue by City Hall (L)* **(P283)** *to the Public Square. See Springfield Public Square (page 23).*]

Continue south on Glenstone.

<u>City 66</u> - Jct. Glenstone & Division.

Evangel College (R), on the site of W.W. II O'Reilly Army Hospital **(P284)**. The old Lily Tulip plant (L) **(P285)**. Silver Saddle Motel (R)(815), originally Baldridge Motor Court **(P286)**. Cross Chestnut Expwy (Business Loop 44) to Jct. St Louis Street. On the (L) by station, a business that was the Manhattan Dinner House **(P287)**. Aerial view of 66 **(P288)**. On the (R) the Rail Haven Motel (Cottage) **(P289)**. Right on St. Louis (City 66) five blocks over the tracks, past an empty lot (R)(1300 block) of the old Corral Drive-In Restaurant **(P290)**, past Dillon's market (L)(1260), site of the Elmhurst Motel **(P291)**, and the Springfield Veterinary Hospital (R)(1213) **(P292)**. Jct. National Ave. Oriental restaurant (R)(1135) that once was Gus Otto's Eat Shop, reviewed by a 1946 AAA guide as "much better than its exterior indicates." Colonial Baking Company (L)(1028) **(P293)**. The old Kentwood Arms Hotel (L)(700) **(P294, P295)**. Abou Ben Adhem Shrine Mosque (R) **(P296)**. Jct. Kimbrough. View of 66 **(P297)**. Lot (L), site of Pierce Bus Terminal **(P298)**. Mercantile Bank (R) (300 block), site of the old USO grounds **(P299)**.

[*NOTE: City 66 (St. Louis Street)* **(P300)** *is now cut off by "Ozark Jubilee Park on Historic Old 66," site of the old Jewell Theatre* **(P301)**.]

Follow curve to Jefferson Ave. Left on Jefferson to Park Central East (St. Louis). Turn right. Colonial Hotel (L) **(P302)**. Woodruff Building (R) **(P303)**. Gilloiz Theatre (R) **(P304, P305)**.

Springfield Public Square **(P306)**. Abundant Life Center (R), once the Fox movie theatre. Exit Square on Park Central West (College St.- old extension of St. Louis).

[*NOTE: College (City 66) is cut off for 1 block.*]

Right on Campbell, left on Olive and curve back into College (City 66). Old Calaboose (L) **(P307)**. 2 miles to Kansas Expwy. Hawkins Milling Co. (L) **(P308)**. Across on the (L), the old Rainbow Garden Court (1930). Ginny Lee's Restaurant, Motel & Pub (L)(2204), originally Rockwood Court **(P309)**. Shamrock Square Motel (L)(2300), built in 1935, now Stanford Square. Melinda Court (L)(2400), once Rock Fountain Court **(P310)**. Jct. Chestnut Expwy. Left. Remains (L)(2846) of Red's Giant Hamburg **(P311)** and the "66" Motel **(P312)**. Trantham's Bait Shop (L), next to what's left of Traveler's Court (3134) **(P313)**.
Jct. Chestnut Expwy & US 160 (West Bypass). (See below.)

2) BYPASS 66.

[*NOTE: This was designated Bypass 66 in 1936.*]

Straight on Kearney (MO 744) 1-1/2 miles, past the Rancho Court (L), once Trail's End Motel **(P269)**, and Hiland Dairy (R)(1133) **(P314)**, to Doling Park **(P315)** turnoff (R)(300) (Robberson St). Traveler's Motel (R) (early 1940s). Jct. West Bypass (US 160). Left, past the Rex Smith Gas Station (R) (originally a "Flying A" station/cafe with cabins in back) that has been operated by the same family since 1932, and under the railroad overpasses (1935) to Jct. Chestnut Expwy.

Jct. Chestnut Expwy & US 160 (West Bypass).
Odometer Notation: (0.0m)

Git 'n' Go station (R), site of the Bypass Terminal Cafe **(P316)**. The Wishing Well Motor Inn (L) **(P316)**. West on Chestnut, past the Best Budget Inn (R)(4433), once the Lone Star Tourist Court **(P317)** and Seven Gables Restaurant (R) **(P318)**, a 2-story building in the 1920s. It exploded and burned in the early 1950s, and was rebuilt, still with a 7-gabled roof. Continue over I-44, past golf course. Homer's Body Shop (R), part of Andy's Modern Rock Cottages **(P319)**. **(4.5m)** This Old House (R) **(P320, P321)**.

1/2 mile on the (L), buildings (L) that were Moore's Sinclair/Texaco filling station and two cabins (idle since the early 1970s). **(6m)** Barnes General Store (L) **(P322, P323)**. Stone buildings on the (R) that were the O'Dell gas station and cafe. **(7m)** Jct. CO. T.

[4 miles to the right is **BOIS D'ARC. The name is French for "wood of the bow," now commonly called "Osage Orange," the strong, pliable hedgeapple tree local Indians used for weapons. From 1847 to 1868, the town name was spelled as it was pronounced, "Bow Dark."**]

Continue 1/2 mile on MO 266. R&J Floral buildings (R) that were Graystone Heights **(P324)**. **(10m)** Farm Rd 59 (R), at an abandoned stretch of Old 66 (L) (FR 140) that crossed Pickerel Creek by a building that was part of Camp Rose **(P325)**.

(11.5m) Jct. Farm Road 45. **PLANO. Probably named for Plano, Texas (now part of Dallas), with which there had been a great deal of trade. A post office from 1895 to 1903.**
Rock residence (L) that was a grocery store/Tydol gas station. 2-story remains (R) of a casket factory/mortuary; later a furniture store.

(15.5m) HALLTOWN. (Pop. 161). **George Hall settled in the area in 1870, opened a store, and in 1879 named the new post office after the storekeeper. In the early 1920s, the town consisted of three grocery stores, a drugstore, variety store, blacksmith shop, garage, and a church. After W.W. II, there were as many as five gas stations included with 15 - 20 businesses. Halltown is now known for its antique shops.** Whitehall Mercantile, Jerry & Thelma White's antique store (R), built (1900) as a grocery with fraternal and community functions upstairs. The old Las Vegas Hotel and barber shop (L) (c.1930), built by Charlie Dammer with silver dollars he had won in Las Vegas. Halltown Flea Market (R) (West's Grocery) (1922). Remodeled building (R) that was Stone's Corner Station (1927), once owned and operated by Ted & Marjorie Stone. Richard's Antiques (R), once a livery and meat packing business, next door to the old Hamilton, Brown Shoe Co. **(P326)**. View of 66 **(P327)**. Bridge over Billies Creek (1923). **(16.5m)** Remains of White City Motel (R) (c.1950), once consisting of 10 cabins with garages encircling an office/residence.

[*NOTE: In the 1950s, towns along US 66 from here to Carthage threatened to sue the government if they lost the "US 66" designation to "I-44," the newly proposed 4-lane interstate highway to be built over Route 66. The highway department made the decision to change the proposed route of I-44 south, following US 166 (completed 1962-1965), thus bypassing this stretch of road. Subsequently, US 66 was rebuilt (1956) to meet new standards, razing many businesses, and, in 1972, lost its "US 66" status anyway, being redesignated MO 96.*]

Continue straight, past MO 96 (L) (MO 266 ends).
(18.5m) PARIS SPRINGS. Named for E.G. Paris, local hotel proprietor, in 1872. The "healing" waters of the nearby springs brought about the formation of the Paris Springs Bottling Co. The town moved 1/2 mile south to its present location, and is now called Paris Springs Junction.

Cobblestone garage and station (R) (c.1926). The old Gay Parita Store (L) (1930), with cafe/grocery, station, and three cabins that rented for $1 - $2 in 1935. Slab stone garage (L) (c.1944). Bridge over Turnback Creek (1923). **(19.5m)** Jct. MO 96 & CO. N. At stop sign, cross MO 96 on CO. N (Old 66). Proceed 1/2 mile, turn right on first road (Farm Road 2062) (Old 66) and over the steel thru-truss bridge (1926) over Johnson Creek.

(20m) SPENCER. Spencer's Store was on the site of the old Johnson's Mill, and in 1868 the post office was named for the store. The existing buildings (R) date to the early 1920s.
Continue on a stretch of original Route 66 surface up the hill 1 mile past a house (L) among the foundation ruins of what was Camp Lookout **(P328)** to Jct. MO 96. Cross over MO 96 and continue west on "outer road" (Old 66) for 2 miles, joining MO 96.

[*NOTE: From here to Carthage there are numerous remains of gas stations/stores and garages along the roadside.*]

(25m) Remodeled buildings (L), once Castle Rock Courts (1931), consisting of a filling station/restaurant and tourist camp.

(25.5m) HEATONVILLE. In 1868 Daniel Heaton laid out a town on his property and named it for Daniel Heaton. The post office was called Heaton from 1872 to 1881.
Treasure Corner (L), once D.L. Morris Garage (1936), built on the site of the old Heaton post office.

(27m) ALBATROSS. A village established in 1926 and named for the Albatross Bus Lines that stopped here. Like other towns on Route 66, Albatross grew with the highway into the 1950s (six gas stations).
Remains of Carver's Cabins (R), with an old station in front. The old Albatross Store (L) (c.1930) with an addition (1949) that is now an auto body shop. Miller's Station (L), once Morgan's DX (c.1945). Jct. MO 39. **(30m)** Group of gray buildings (L) that was the Welcome Inn (c.1940), once a tavern (then restaurant) with cabins in back.

(31m) PHELPS. Named for Colonel Bill Phelps, a famous local attorney for the MoPac Railroad, and the lobbyist who obtained a post office for the town in 1857.
What's left of Bill's Station (R) (c.1926). Henson Building (R) (1924) (now a residence), once with a cafe, store & barber shop, with rental rooms upstairs.

(35m) RESCUE. In the late 1800s, a family traveling out West had their wagon break down. Locals took them in for the few days it took for repairs. Afterward, the family said they were lucky to have been "rescued." The area's well-deserved reputation accounted for the new post office's name in 1897.
Cabins, lodge and station (R), built by a Mr. & Mrs. Roy Rogers in the 1920s (not that one!); later Reeds Cabins. **(36m)** Remains of Shady Side Camp (R) **(P329)**.

(38.5m) PLEW. For years known as Plewtite, the town was named for a local family in 1893.

(40m) LOG CITY (L) and **(40.5m) STONE CITY (L).** These towns were known for their popular resorts frequented by many from Carthage and the surrounding area, and named for their materials of construction.
Across from Log City (P330) are the old cabins of the rival Forest Park Camp (P331).

(43.5m) AVILLA. (Pop. 146). Laid out by D.S. Holman and A.L. Love in 1858, and named for Avilla, Indiana, their hometown.

(50.5m) Old 66 is visible on the (R).

[*NOTE:* **(51.5m)** *Original US 66 crossed to the left near the site of an old filling station (R), (follow the power poles); New 66 (MO 96) went straight.*]

Left, then right on Old 66 1 mile. On the (L), across from a trailer park, is a stone building (that sold barbeque) associated with the old Sunset Drive-In (early 1950s-late 1960s). The ticket booth and concession stand (now a converted barn) still stand. Red Rock Apartments (R), originally White Court (P332). Kellogg Lake Park. Right.
Jct. MO 96. Lake Shore Motel (R) (P333). Across MO 96, Kel-Lake Motel (P334). Left onto MO 96 (Central Ave - City 66) 1-1/2 miles over Spring River bridges (1923), and the balustrade bridge (1934) over the Frisco tracks, veering right to Jct. Garrison & Central (2nd light). (See below.)

CARTHAGE. (Pop. 10,747). Established in 1842, the town was named for ancient Carthage, a model of democracy. Carthage was the capitol of the marble industry at the turn of the century. The Missouri State Capitol, U.S. Capitol, and even the White House are all faced with the stone. Carthage was also the home of Belle Starr, the notorious "Bandit Queen."
In town, the Square and the Jasper County Courthouse (P335), both on the National Register of Historic Places.

Jct. Garrison & Central. Left on Garrison, past the Boots Court (R) (P336) and the old Boots Drive-In (P337) across the street, now an insurance business. Right on Oak Street 1 mile to Municipal Park (L) (1937). Jct. stop signs.

[*NOTE: Old 66 went straight, behind the 66 Drive-In, but is now cut off by US 71.*]

Veer left, past the front of 66 Drive-In Theatre (R) (1945), able to accommodate over 650 cars. Cross over US 71. Left on Leggett Rd (Old 66) 1-1/2 miles to the "double-arch" Center Creek bridge (1926), past Lakeside Park (P338), to stop sign (Carterville Cemetery). Left (Pine) to Main Street (stop sign).

CARTERVILLE. (Pop. 2,013). **Named for J.L. Carter, one of the men who laid out the town in 1875. During W.W. I Carterville was a prosperous city of 12,000, but then the mines shut down.**
Right on Main. Continue through town and the abandoned mines and piles of slag (chat - the waste from lead and zinc mines) **(P339)**.

WEBB CITY. (7,449). **After "discovering" lead in his cornfield in 1873, John C. Webb created a mine, made money, and platted the town later named for him.**
Veer left onto Broadway. Remains (R) of the wood frame Daugherty Street Filling Station (c. 1930). Continue on Broadway, past the Webb City Bank, to Webb. Ahead is the Professional Plaza building, once Civic Drive-In Cafe **(P340)**. Left on Webb 1/2 block to Broadway. Right to Jct. Jefferson Avenue (900 block).

JOPLIN. (Pop. 40,866). **Named to honor the Rev. Harris G. Joplin, who established the first Methodist congregation in Jasper County in 1840. By an act of the state legislature in 1873 (brought about by some local "skirmishes"), the communities of East Joplin, West Joplin, Murphysburg, and Union City were merged under the name Joplin.** A few miles to the southwest, at the juncture of Missouri, Kansas and Oklahoma, is the "Tri-State Spook Light," a still unexplained phenomenon dating back before the turn of the century. Joplin was a large lead and zinc mining area in the 19th century, and there have been numerous cave-ins of the city streets (caused by a labyrinth of abandoned mine tunnels under the city) creating various US 66 routes through town, all ending at Jct. Main & West 7th Streets. (Main Street was, during the old mining days, a rather bawdy place, as witnessed by an ad for the old House of Lords, saying it offers "...fine cuisine, gambling, and 'soiled doves.' " The site is now a city park.)

1) CITY 66.
Jct. Broadway & Jefferson. Left on Jefferson.

[NOTE: Jefferson is soon cut off by MacArthur Blvd (MO 171).]

Right on MacArthur 1 block to Jct. Madison Ave. Left. McDonald's (410 Madison), on the site of the old Ozark Motel **(P341)**. South on Madison. Just before the Oaklawns office building (R)(2700N) was the site of Fenix Ultra Modern Court (2710N) **(P342)**. Continue to Zora Ave. (1st stop light). On the (L), Coach's Corner, the site of Lincrest Court **(P343)**. Right on Zora to 2600 block, left on Florida ("Mathews" on the right) to Jct. Utica (2200 block). 2-story building (L) that was the Royal Heights Apartments (c.1930), then the Joplin Little Theater for awhile. Right on Utica. Barber shop (L) that was the Shamrock Inn, Gas Station/Cafe (c.1930). Angle left onto Euclid to stop sign, left on St. Louis, right on Broadway (stop sign). Left onto Main Street (MO 43). View of 66 **(P344)**. Office (L)(419), once Bob Miller's Restaurant **(P345)**. Jct. Main & West 7th Street.(See page 28.)

2) ALTERNATE 66.

Jct. Broadway & Jefferson. Continue straight on Broadway, angle left onto Powell Street, right on MacArthur (MO 171) 1-1/2 miles. Left on Main Street (MO 43) 5 miles to the 300 block. View of 66 (P344). Office (L)(419), once Bob Miller's Restaurant (P345). Jct. Main & West 7th Street. (See below.)

3) BYPASS 66.

Jct. Broadway & Jefferson. Continue straight on Broadway. Left on Madison Ave to Jct. MacArthur Blvd (MO 171). McDonald's (410 Madison), on the site of the old Ozark Motel (P341). Straight on Madison (Range Line). Just before the Oaklawns office building (R)(2700N) was the site of Fenix Ultra Modern Court (2710N) (P342). Continue to Zora (1st stop light). On the (L), Coach's Corner station on the site of Lincrest Court (2601N) (P343). Continue straight. Jct. Range Line & 4th. Ben Franklin Crafts parking lot (L), site of the Twin Oaks Court (401S) (P346). Jct. Range Line & 7th. (R) corner, the site of the old Elms Motel (628S) (347).

[Straight here on Range Line 1/2 block to The Colonel's Restaurant (R) (P348).]

West on 7th, past Bob Owen Auto Center (L)(1902) that occupies the site of East 7th Street Motel (P349), to Jct. Main & West 7th Street.

Jct. Main & West 7th Street.

West on 7th (MO 66) 2 blocks, past a station & tire store (R) that was originally Ozark Filling Station (1925) to Wal-Mart (R)(1717), site of the Koronado Hotel Kourts, "Our Rooms and Coffee Shops are Air Conditioned by Refrigeration." West 7th St. Apts (R)(2207), once Little King's Hotel Court, built in the 1930s and advertising "Good eats close by." Pride Motors office (R)(2403) that was part of Castle Kourt (P350). Next door, the 66 Pit Stop Lounge (R), at one time Dixie Lee's Dine & Dance Bar (1930). Schifferdecker Park (R) (P351). Continue west on MO 66 2 miles to "Old Route 66 Next Right" sign. Right. Remains of Shady Rest Motel (L), and Gillead's Barbeque (L) (c.1945). Liquor store (R) that was Gray & Archer Filling Station (c.1925). State Line Bar & Grill (R) (c.1925), originally a restaurant/honky-tonk, was the first business to greet those from Kansas when it was "dry."

Kansas State Line.

(P1) MUNICIPAL BRIDGE. Used as an alternate route across the Mississippi River, the Municipal Bridge (1917-1981) was built at a cost of $6,000,000. This view is towards East St. Louis, IL. (Renamed MacArthur Bridge after W.W. II.)

New McKinley Bridge, largest electric bridge in the world, St. Louis, Mo.

(P2) MCKINLEY BRIDGE. Built in 1910 for trains and livestock (with outside lanes added later for cars and trucks), at the time it was the largest electric bridge in the world.

29

New

JEFFERSON

HOTEL

ST. LOUIS

MISSOURI

(P3) JEFFERSON HOTEL. Now the Jefferson Arms Apartments, the hotel was completed in time for the 1904 St. Louis World's Fair. With 800 rooms, it was the "largest and most modern in the city."

(P4) CIVIL COURTS BUILDING (1930). This "new" courthouse (Susan's favorite!) was built to replace the one still standing at the east end of Memorial Plaza, by the Arch. The "temple" on top (housing the law library) is a replica of the tomb (mausoleum) of King Mausolus of Asia Minor (352 B.C.), one of the Seven Wonders of the Ancient World. This view is east along Market Street (early 66), with City Hall among the trees on the right.

City Hall, St. Louis, Mo.

(P5) CITY HALL. Constructed during the years 1890-1904, the building is a replica of the old Hotel deVille (City Hall) of Paris. The statue in front is of Ulysses S. Grant, Civil War hero and 18th President, who married a St. Louis girl, Julia Dent, and lived in the area for a number of years.

(P6) ST. FRANCIS DE SALES CHURCH (1895). Its 300-foot steeple is the tallest in the city. On the National Register of Historic Places, this is but one of the many beautiful and historic churches of St. Louis.

(P7) EDMOND'S. This restaurant, "Home of Unusual Sea Foods" (and recommended by Duncan Hines), advertised the "Largest variety of seafood in the Middle West. Shipments arrive daily from all coasts. Specializing in Maine Lobster - Steaks - Chicken. Air conditioned during summer season." A 1946 AAA directory called Edmonds "One of the best."

(P8) SHANGRI-LA. "The Club Beautiful," the Shangri-La offered chicken, steaks, and "delicious Italian foods." The special in 1946 was a "Deluxe Century Steak Dinner $2.75." "On your day or evening out - Visit Shangri-La First."

(P9) TED DREWES FROZEN CUSTARD. Started in 1929, this family-run business has been on Route 66 since 1941. (Although this photo is from the 1970s, the building looked the same from 1941 to 1985, when expansion to the east was completed.) The original sign still stands at the corner of the west lot. One of St. Louis' most well-known landmarks.

(P10) CORAL COURT. On the National Register of Historic Places, this Art Deco motor court (1941-1993), with its fully enclosed individual garages, gained a racy reputation as a "no-tel motel." Plans are underway to restore many of the units and create a Route 66 "Way Station/Museum."

(P11) WAYSIDE AUTO COURT (1940). Now boasting "A Phone In Every Room," these brick cottages with 35 rooms offered a "private tiled bath in each unit, hot and cold water, maid service. Beauty-Rest mattresses." According to a 1946 AAA travel directory, "One of the better courts."

(P12) CHIPPEWA MOTEL. Originally 13 freestanding units called "tourist cottages." Travelers were offered inside hot and cold running water and access to the community toilets and shower for $1.50 - $3 a night. Since remodeled, the Chippewa is now apartments.

(P13) DUPLEX MOTEL (1937). This was one of the first tourist camps along Watson Road. Originally 11 freestanding brick cottages with private toilets and showers, hot and cold inside running water, steam heat, fans and radios, all for only $2.50 - $4 per night. By 1946 it had grown to 24 rooms with "Free City Maps."

(P14) 66 AUTO COURT. A 1946 AAA directory lists 30 rooms with baths for $2.50 - $3.50 a night, calling it "pleasant." The court mentioned "Hot Water Heat - Insulated Rooms - Innerspring Mattresses. St. Louis' Finest Modern Auto Court. Why Spend The Night in The City."

(P15) MOTEL ROYAL. This "Travelers Paradise" had 60 rooms all fronting on its wide expanse of private parkway. In addition to radiant heat, the Royal had "attached garage, glass and tile shower, radio in every room. Recommended by AAA and Duncan Hines."

(P16) THE OAKS MOTEL. "16 rooms with private tile bath in each room - hot and cold water - porter and maid service - Unit controlled gas heat." The liquor store featured "Tobacco, candy and novelties."

(P17) BLUE HAVEN AUTO COURT. Starting as a home with "rooms for rent" in the early 1940s, it grew to 24 single units with "carport" garages. Sol Schlansky, who lived in and operated the Blue Haven from 1955 to 1975, also raised chickens for his "market."

(P18) BLUE BONNET COURT (1938). The court had 16 brick cottages "individually heated with modern oil heat, the fumes of which are carried off by vents. A place of refinement at moderate prices" ($2 - $3). "Open all year, day and night."

Twin-Six Auto Court, 10,230 Hwy. 66, St. Louis 22, Mo.

(P19) TWIN-SIX AUTO COURT (c.1940). These "Ultra-modern Tourist Cottages," with coffee shop, dining room and lounge, were built by the Sinwell brothers. The garages were added after W.W. II. Around 1969 A.W. Aschinger purchased the property, tearing the court down in 1986.

(P20) WATSON/KIRKWOOD CLOVERLEAF. This was the first "cloverleaf" interchange west of the Mississippi River. Built of pink granite in 1932 (restructured in 1980) to handle the traffic of the new "southern" version of City Route 66 (Watson Rd) at its junction with Bypass 66 (Kirkwood Rd). The view is to the south on Kirkwood toward the town of Festus.

(P21) WESTWARD MOTEL. Built in 1953 by architect Bernard McMahon and partners, this "western style" motel had 26 "Luxurious Rooms. Controlled Air Conditioning. Complimentary Coffee Bar. One of the nation's best." Mr. McMahon still remembers the horror of having only *one* guest on opening night!

(P22) SPENCER'S GRILL. Originally a grocery store, Spencer's is shown here after it was converted to a restaurant (1947) by William Spenser, who lived upstairs. It has been run continuously as Spencer's Grill since, even retaining the original sign!

(P23) MISSOURI PACIFIC DEPOT (1893). Built on the site of the original station (1851), this depot is on the National Register of Historic Places.

(P24) NELSON'S CAFE. This cafe, offering Sealtest ice cream and "Chicken - Steaks," was next door to the Park Plaza Court. Owned and operated by a Dr. and Mrs. Meyer into the 1950s, the restaurant was later known as the "Viking."

(P25) PARK PLAZA COURT. When this photo was taken (mid-1950s), the Park Plaza advertised "85 lovely, Air-Conditioned Rooms & Suites. Room Phones, T-V, Room Service. A Nelson Restaurant on Premises." The motel grew to 135 rooms.

(P26) SYLVAN BEACH PARK. Built in the 1930s, this privately operated amusement and recreational park on the Meramec River grew to include the restaurant/lounge and cabins scattered among the public picnic grounds, baseball diamonds, and swimming pool. "We Cater to Parties and Picnics. We Never Close." Razed in 1954 with the construction of the new US 66 dual bridges. (The park and pool remain.)

DUDLEY'S CABINS AND SERVICE
HIGHWAY 66, 9 MILES WEST OF ST. LOUIS
AIR CONDITIONED, RADIO IN EVERY CABIN, VALLEY PARK, MO.

(P27) DUDLEY'S CABINS AND SERVICE. These "All Modern Cabins" with private baths were on the Henry Shaw Gardenway. The cabins and Mobilgas Station were built in the early 1930s (Dudley was a "moonshiner") and later became the Jam Inn in the 50s. (Its owner later retired in the 1980s and moved to Las Vegas.) It was razed for Maritz Co. expansion.

TRAV-O-TEL DELUXE COURT
ST. LOUIS, MO.
OFFICIAL AAA COURT

STEAM HEAT
MEMBER NATIONAL
TRAV-O-TEL-SYSTEM

ELECTRIC FANS
U. S. HIGHWAY No. 66
11 MILES WEST of ST. LOUIS

(P28) TRAV-O-TEL DELUXE COURT. The 16 brick cottages were near the junction of US 66 and the old Antire Road (from the north). It offered "Steam Heat - Electric Fans - Private Bath - Broadloom Rugs - Closed Locked Garages," and private cooking facilities for only $2 - $4 a night in 1938. According to a 1939 AAA guide, "One of the finest courts to be found in the St. Louis area."

(P29) VIEW OF 66 - ST. LOUIS COUNTY. Trees being planted by homeless labor along US 66 (1934). For 30 miles, from the St. Louis city limits to the Shaw Arboretum in Gray Summit, Route 66 was designated Henry Shaw Gardenway to honor the man who founded the world famous Missouri Botanical Gardens (1859). Bordered by a collection of native trees and shrubs, the memorial boulevard has since lost much of its beauty to urban growth and highway expansion.

(P30) VIEW OF 66 - ST. LOUIS COUNTY. Looking west on 4-lane US 66 (Henry Shaw Gardenway) a couple miles east of Times Beach (October, 1953). The highway sign reads "Slow 40 Miles."

Steiny's Inn, Famous for Fine Food

Overlooking the Meramec, Highway 66, Eureka, Mo.

(P31) STEINY'S INN. Once a popular tourist stop (in 1938 the 10 "cottages" rented for $1.50 - $3 a night), the inn was built by Edward Steinberg in the early 1930s across the Meramec River from the new town of Times Beach. It became the Bridgehead Inn, later Galley West. (The restaurant was closed in the mid-1980s.) The remodeled building is now occupied by the Environmental Protection Agency.

(P32) THE AL-PAC RESTAURANT (c.1942). Named for the nearby towns of Allenton and Pacific, the restaurant was "Home of Good Food." Outside signs offered "Baked Ham," and "C.P. Root Beer."

(P33) THE AL-PAC (c.1942). After an adjoining motel was added, you could still "Enjoy Breakfast, Lunch or Dinner in our beautiful cedar dining room."

(P34) BEACON COURT (c.1946). "10 modern, inviting, tastefully decorated cottages. Tile baths, garages, air conditioned, automatic hot water heat. Reservations held until 6 P.M. Restaurant next door."

"RED CEDAR INN"
28 Miles West of St. Louis, Mo.   Delicious Foods   Highway No. 66

(P35) RED CEDAR INN (1934). Built by James and Bill Smith using logs cut from their family farm. (The bar addition was made in 1935.) At one time with Mobilgas pumps, the inn specialized in "Chicken, Steak, Frog" dinners. The Red Cedar is still owned and operated by the Smith family.

(P36) JENSEN POINT. This scenic overlook (1938 - no longer accessible) was named to honor Lars Peter Jensen, first director of the Shaw Arboretum in Gray Summit. It was part of the Henry Shaw Gardenway plan. (Efforts are underway to relocate the pavilion.)

(P37) VIEW OF 66 - PACIFIC. Silica (fine white sand) mining in this area started in the 1870s. These "caves" were exposed when US 66 construction crews "sheared" the face of the hills back to make way for the new road (1932).

(P38) CAVE CAFE. Built just after completion of the new "southern route" US 66 through town (1933), and named for the "caves" across the road created by the mines, the Cave Cafe was owned by Ralph Martin from 1943 to 1987. Like other US 66 gas stations, oil companies like Gulf leased the station for a fee of one-cent-a-gallon pumped! At times the cafe had been operated as a tavern. (The service bays were added in the early 1960s.)

(P39) TRAIL'S END MOTEL (1945). These "modern" heated units with showers were later connected; the large, vertical "MOTEL" sign was added by then-owners Willard & Bernice Haley after I-44 opened (1965).

(P40) MUNICIPAL AUDITORIUM (1934). Containing an opera house (in front) and a modern sports arena, in 1943 the facility was renamed Kiel Auditorium, for Mayor Henry W. Kiel ("keel"). It was built on the site of a tavern where Frankie Baker (in 1899) shot her lover, inspiring the song "Frankie and Johnny."

(P41) UNION STATION (1894). At one time this was the largest and busiest railway station in the world, with its Grand Hall covering 8800 sq. ft. Said to be modeled after the walled medieval city of Carcassone of southern France, the station (with its "Terminal Hotel") has been restored to its original magnificence and is now a hotel/shopping mall/entertainment complex. Designated a National Historic Landmark, it is truly awesome!

(P42) 9-MILE HOUSE. Called Trainwreck Saloon since 1982, it was once the 9-Mile House (1890), a tavern and railroad boardinghouse that was nine miles from St. Louis, proudly serving the National Brewery Company's Griesedieck Brother's beer. It was operated as Porta's Tavern for 50 years (1932-1982).

(P43) DIEM'S TAVERN/STORE. Now the Village Bar, the building was originally Joseph Diem's tavern and store (c.1895). This view (early 1900s) shows Joe's 2-story house (1875 - still standing) next door.

(P44) TOURIST HOTEL. Built in the 1880s and shown here as the 1920s remodeled Weidner Tourist Hotel (with a log cabin out back for "rowdies" to stay). Demand waned after the 1933 "southern route" of US 66 was completed, and again after W.W. II. It then became the Weidner private residence.

OFFICIAL PROGRAM

PRICE
25¢
Pay no more

C.C.PYLE
217
L.A.-N.Y. RACE

C.C.Pyle's
First Annual
INTERNATIONAL-TRANS-CONTINENTAL
FOOT RACE
LOS ANGELES
TO
NEW YORK
1928

(P45) TRANS-CONTINENTAL FOOT RACE. Charles C. Pyle's First Annual International-Trans-Continental Foot Race (dubbed the "Bunion Derby") was intended to promote the new US 66 Highway. 275 runners took off from Los Angeles for Chicago, then New York. Englishman Peter Gavuzzi reached this 54th control point in the lead on Thursday, April 26, 1928. (His time for the 45-1/2 miles from Sullivan was 6 hours, 11 minutes.) The 55 runners who finished averaged around six miles per hour, with the $25,000 1st prize going to Andy Payne, second at the Ellisville stop.

(P46) POND INN. Built as a tavern in 1875, it is now a French restaurant.

TOURIST CABINS LOOKING TOWARD MAIN BUILDING —BIG CHIEF CABIN HOTEL

(P47) BIG CHIEF CABIN HOTEL. With its 62 "large, attractively furnished, steam-heated, modern fireproof cabins" ($1.50 dbl), 24-hour Conoco service station, tavern, and restaurant with dance floor, the Big Chief (late 1920s) was a landmark on early Route 66. The cabins have been razed, but the restaurant/office is being renovated.

(P48) BIG CHIEF HOTEL. This placemat/menu is "For Tourists Who Care." After the new "southern route" of US 66 was completed (1933), US 66/US 50 became just US 50 (MO 100). ("Missouri Highway 77, Denny Road" later became Lindbergh Blvd.)

(P49) FOX CREEK GARAGE (c.1922). The Fox Creek Garage & Ford Dealership ("Ford Work A Specialty") later became Ed Schott Pontiac (1927). It is now used as a warehouse.

(P50) MOTOR INN. Built by Rudy (R.J.) & Edna Dehn around 1927 (photo c.1929), the restaurant offered hamburgers for 10 cents and roast beef, pork, or baked ham sandwiches for 15 cents. The business was torn down in the 1960s.

(P51) SUMMIT COTTAGE. This cottage/restaurant/Texaco gas station (1930) featured "Good Home Cooking." The pumps, like most others of this period, were capable of holding around 10 gallons "hand pumped" by an attendant to fill the "glass." Car tanks were filled through a "gravity" system.

CHAIN OF ROCKS BRIDGE
St. Louis, Mo.

(P52) CHAIN OF ROCKS BRIDGE. "Chain of Rocks" refers to the natural ridge of rocks that deters Mississippi River travel during low water. (There is now a bypass canal.) Construction of the bridge (1929-1977) was started by an individual who was forced by the government to "bend" the bridge to prevent blockage of water flow into Intake Tower No. 2. Lacking ownership of the land at the new destination, he declared bankruptcy. The city of Madison, IL then bought the bridge.

(P53) CHAIN OF ROCKS BRIDGE/FUN FAIR PARK. This view of the bridge shows Fun Fair Park on a bluff high above Route 66. (Also seen are the two intake towers in the river.) The park, known variously as Chain of Rocks Amusement Park and Riverview Park, was a popular spot for weary Route 66 travelers. It was built on land that had been proposed for use as the site of the 1904 St. Louis World's Fair (held instead in Forest Park). This postcard was mailed in 1947.

(P54) JOHN B. MYERS HOUSE. Designed by John Myers, the construction of the home (1869) was overseen by his widow Adelaide. The house and barn are both on the National Register of Historic Places. Restored, they now contain antique shops and a restaurant.

Route 66 Association

Of Missouri

For Membership Information
Box 8117   St. Louis, MO 63156   (314) 982-5500

(P55) AERIAL VIEW OF 66 - HAZELWOOD. This view (c.1950) is to the west, showing Lindbergh Blvd (Bypass 66) running left to right (south to north), with the old Lambert Airport terminal on the far left, Ford Motor Co. (1948) in the center, the Airport Motel across Lindbergh, and 66 curving sharply to the right (east) towards the Mississippi River (I-270 "covered" this stretch of Bypass 66 in 1961).

57

(P56) AIRPORT MOTEL. Built by the Holtzman family after new Bypass 66 was designated (1936), this motel, with four rooms in the front, two in rear, and four in another building in back, has been in continuous operation since. A 1946 AAA directory rated the motel "Very nice." (The front unit on the right is now a barber shop.)

(P57) LAMBERT AIR FIELD. Now called Lambert-St. Louis International Airport (with a new terminal on the south side), originally (1920) it was called Lambert Flying Field, with its terminal on the west facing Lindbergh Blvd. Named for Major Albert Bond Lambert, owner of the air field and one of Charles Lindbergh's original backers for his historic 1927 flight across the Atlantic in the "Spirit of St. Louis."

(P58) STANLEY COUR-TEL (1950). Built by Stanley Williams, this motel had "Comfortable hot water heat" (steam) with showers in each unit. America's original seven astronauts stayed here during their 6-month training at nearby McDonnell Douglas, builder of the Mercury space capsule.

(P59) AIR-O-WAY COURTS. Built in the early 1930s, the original four "steamheated Permastone cottages" housing 16 units still stand (with remodeled connecting rooms upstairs). "City Certified water. Spring Air Mattresses, Blond Oak furniture. Radio in every room." Then-owner Harold Jones dropped the "O" from the name in the 1970s for better name recognition.

(P60) SUNSET ACRES MOTEL. "Ultra-modern accommodations. Airform mattresses and pillows. Mengel Furniture. Convenient location and moderate rates." Built around 1950, it was razed prior to the construction of Northwest Plaza in 1965.

(P61) KING BROS. MOTEL. Throughout its "infamous" history, the motel advertised "Modern units, Simmons furnished. Hot water heat. All tile showers." In 1946 its 33 rooms (all with baths) rented for $3 - $3.50 a night for two.

(P62) OFFICIAL WEIGHT STATION. This official Missouri weight station (c.1942) weighed 54,000 trucks in 1942. (In 1992, the nearby I-44 St. Clair station weighed 380,000!) It was located on the present site of the new Diamonds Restaurant, across from Shaw Arboretum. This one scale was used for both east and westbound trucks, creating frequent traffic pileups. (The truck in front was owned by Milligan Grocery of St. Louis.) Nice uniforms!

(P63) COZY DINE CAFE. This cafe and Shell station was operated by Clifford & Verna Weirich (who had worked for Clifford prior to their marriage) from the late 1930s to the mid-1940s.

(P64) GARDENWAY MOTEL (c.1945). Named for the Henry Shaw Gardenway (Old 66), this motel was built at its western terminus. The first units were constructed by Louis Elkelkamp a short distance from his family's home. The motel grew to 41 rooms, all with tile baths. Wonderful sign!

(P65) WAYSIDE FARMERS MARKET/MINGLE INN. Started (1946) by Wilbert & Ruth Meyer as a "one-quonset hut" apple market, they soon sold fresh fruit and produce to locals and travelers. A "front" was added in 1952. ("Quonset huts" were constructed for the U.S. Navy in 1942 at Quonset Point Naval Air Station in Rhode Island.) Next door, the 2-story Mingle home offered a cafe and barber shop downstairs, rental rooms up.

THE DIAMONDS RESTAURANT AND CABINS

JUNCION 50·66·100   VILLA RIDGE, MO.

(P66) THE DIAMONDS. Built in 1927, and rebuilt after a fire in 1948, the Diamonds was constructed in the shape of a baseball diamond to fit the wedge-shaped lot.. Billed as the "World's Largest Roadside Restaurant," at one time it included 25 cottages (across old MO 100), swimming pool and first aid station. "Known from coast to coast for fine foods and courteous service." The restaurant moved east along I-44 to its present location in 1967, retaining its sign.

Sunset Motel

U. S. HIGHWAYS 66 AND 50

38 MILES WEST OF ST. LOUIS, MO.

(P67) SUNSET MOTEL. This motel (built of buff-colored brick) has both front and rear entrances to each unit, and appear (with original sign) as built in the 1940s. The motel advertised "12 Units - 12 Baths - Panel Ray Heat - Beautyrest Mattresses - Air-Conditioned - Quiet."

AMERICAN INN HIGHWAY 50 AND 66, VILLA RIDGE, MO.

(P68) AMERICAN INN (c.1930). The stone building was the garage/station, and the log cabin housed a private residence upstairs and a restaurant down, famous for their Sunday chicken dinners.

Pin Oak Motel
VILLA RIDGE, MO.

(P69) PIN OAK MOTEL (c.1940). Now U-Store-It units, originally there was a small cluster of cottages with attached carports, later enclosed. Prior to conversion to a storage facility there were 28 "clean, ultra-modern units, with Stewart-Warner Sar-Aire heaters," billing itself as "A Better Court For Better People."

(P70) "THE TWIN BRIDGES." This view of the old "Twin Bridges" over the Bourbeuse River shows the westbound Route 66 lane (1935) on the right (now the I-44 outer road bridge) and the eastbound (1940) on the left. Westbound 3-lane 66 narrowed into two lanes through the bridge. The signs to the right read "Bourbeuse River," and "Do Not Park On Bridge."

(P71) HALL'S PLACE (c.1930). Shown are Frank Hall's 2-story house (center), store, restaurant, and Sinclair gas station next to Route 66. The outer road for 4-lane New 66 razed the station building, but the house remains.

(P72) LE CLAIRE MOTORS. The Reed cousins built this house and restaurant around 1937. George LeClaire later created a garage and Phillips 66 station selling package liquors. The sliding doors have been replaced, and a new front built to enclose the entrance as well as the entry to the residence upstairs (which, after being sold, "earned" a rather notorious reputation in later years).

Johnson's Mo-Tel — Cabins— on U.S. 66 — St. Clair, Mo.
Country Ham & Chicken Dinners—Home Style Cooking

(P73) JOHNSON'S MO-TEL CABINS (c.1940). Built by Charlie & Liza Johnson, the front building (since added to) served as the office/dining and living quarters, with cabins in back. The Johnson's had three sons in the Army Air Corps, and Liza was known to never turn down a serviceman's request for a room and/or dinner, no matter the time of night! (According to this postcard, they specialized in Country Ham & Chicken "Dinnners")

(P74) ART'S MO-TEL CABINS (c.1940). The Johnson's Mo-tel was operated under the name Art's Mo-Tel Cabins for about a year, then Johnson's again. In the middle 1950s, Charlie Johnson and his son Robert left this business and built the Skylark Motel west of town.

(P75) HI SPOT INN. This restaurant (with family living quarters in back) was opened by a Mr. Kemper as the first business on US 66 that "bypassed" St. Clair in 1927. (Old Springfield Road, MO 14, went through the downtown area.)

(P76) CHUCK WAGON CAFE. The cafe was originally a Conoco gas station built in the late 1920s. The St. Clair Chronicle building (now shops) was at one time a Ford dealership.

(P77) HARTY'S DINE-O-TEL. A tavern and diner with rooms upstairs, this establishment (with "Deluxe Dining Service"), built for Roger Harty around 1937, claimed to be the "Home of Chicken in the Hay."

(P78) SHADY SHELL. Built by Chris Dall in 1927, the Shell station/garage was operated by Almond (his son) and Mildred Dall until 1931. There were three tourist cabins in back, named "Bluebird," "Oriole," and "Robin;" also, a miniature golf course (with sawdust fairways). The groceries/refreshment stand (R) was operated by Al's brother Clarence.

(P79) RITTER AUTO SALVAGE. The Shady Shell garage later became Berkel & Ritter, then Ritter Auto Salvage (during W.W. II). Pictured is Donna, wife of Jack, one of owner Arthur B. Ritter's sons.

(P80) RITTER & SONS GARAGE. The 2-story addition was added to the business in 1947. The Ritters also built a playground/park for customers. It included a shuffleboard, merry-go-round, and picnic tables with barbeque pits. The garage is currently operated by sons Jerome and Danny. In the background is Harty's Dine-O-Tel.

(P81) ST. CLAIR MOTEL. Built in the early 1940s, the St. Clair provided "Ultra Modern Rooms. Radio - T.V. - Air Cond. - Electric Heating - Tubs - Showers." At various times, the St. Clair has been owned and operated by Fred & Mary Leen, Faye Hermling, and Walter & Kitty Crumbaker.

(P82) SUNSET INN. Built in the late 1920s as Arch Bart's station, the Sunset was originally where the I-44 westbound lanes are now, facing old US 66 (I-44 eastbound). This Sinclair station/restaurant served "Home Baked Ham" and "Delicious Coffee." The Sunset also had four cabins (L) that rented for $1 - $2 in 1938.

(P83) SCULLY'S SUNSET INN. After the business became Scully's (who had been chef at Busch's Grove, a still-popular St. Louis eating establishment), the cabins were replaced with a restaurant expansion. A 1946 AAA directory reported Scully's a "popular dining place." When new lanes were added to US 66 (c.1952), the station and original restaurant were torn down, the restaurant expansion was moved to the outer road, and a motel was built on the property below.

DISPLAY OF OZARK ROCK CURIOS ON HIGHWAY 66 NEAR ST. CLAIR, MO

(P84) OZARK ROCK CURIOS. Run by a Mr. Woodcock (who lived on the property) this was one of the first "souvenir" stands of its kind on US 66 (late 1920s). After the "Free Admission," one could fill 'er up at the Phillips 66 pumps. The business was on the north side of Route 66 that became "covered" by eastbound I-44, moving 1/4 mile west to existing house.

(P85) LERONEY'S. This restaurant ("A Nice Place to Eat") specialized in a "Tender Fried Chicken Plate" for 35 cents. Built around 1930 and known as Bracket's Place, new owner Ed Leroney expanded to include a Texaco service station/grocery store, dancehall, and tourist camp. (The six cabins rented for $1.25 - $2 in 1939.) It burned down after lunch on a Sunday in the late 1940s.

(P86) OZARK COURT (c.1930). Originally this site was owned by a retired policeman from St. Louis (a Mr. Duke) who, as a Justice of the Peace with his two deputies, created what was known as a "speed trap" town with a "kangaroo court." This later building group once had a garage, office/filling station, cabins and cafe, selling souvenirs and pottery. Old 66 is to the left. The sign was relocated after loss of access to the highway.

OZARK SOUVENIRS AT THE "TEPEE"
55 Miles West of St. Louis, Mo.   Highway No. 66   175 Miles East of Springfield

(P87) THE TEEPEE. This souvenir stand was run by a fella called "Indian Joe" who lived in back. In addition to the pottery, he advertised "Cards - Letters Mailed Here." When his business burned in the late 1930s, his clothes caught on fire prompting him to jump into his cistern well. Volunteer firefighters found him not burned to death, but drowned!

16
All Approved
🛆🛆🛆
Modern
Cabins
24 Hr. Cafe

BENSONS

BENSON'S   TOURIST   CITY

7 Miles
West
of
St. Clair, Mo.
U. S. Hiway 66

(P88) **BENSON'S TOURIST CITY** (c.1937). This "city" (owned by Mr. & Mrs. Lewis J. Benson) had a 24-hour cafe/office and Mobilgas station (the existing building in front), a wash house, restrooms, power house, and 16 "all approved AAA modern cabins." (A 1938 Shell tourist directory listed rates as $1.00 to $1.75, with private kitchen facilities, but no dishes!) Their motto? "Your Home Away From Home." Later known as Del-Crest.

MOTEL MERAMEC . . . U.S. Hwy. 66 . . . Stanton, Missouri

WE SERVE
CHICKEN DINNERS

MOTEL MERAMEC
CABINS

OFFICE

VACANCIES

(P89) **MOTEL MERAMEC.** This home, converted into a "motel," advertised "Clean modern cabins and rooms - Dining room in connection - Strictly home cooking. We Serve Chicken Dinners." It later became Kovac's Restaurant/Motel, famous for their chicken & dumplings.

(P90) AERIAL VIEW OF 66 - STANTON. View (c.1965) to the east toward St. Clair. Stanton Motel (L) of the 4-lane New 66 (1954), (R) of the outer road (original 66), the Okay Motel, an old Stuckey's (now Antique Toy Museum), Jesse James Museum (with a corral behind for "shoot-outs"), the Hammer Store (razed for I-44 on-ramp), and by the tracks, the Effie & Louis Wurzburger Place, once providing great food, and gambling in the 1930s (now Appolo Fireworks).

ENTRANCE TO MERAMEC CAVE   STANTON MO.

(P91) MERAMEC CAVERNS. Opened in 1935 by Lester Dill, the "originator" of the bumper sticker. Called "Jesse James Hideout," this became the best known tourist attraction on Route 66. The entrance contained parking space for 300 cars and a large dance floor, now occupied by shops. Over 26 miles of underground passages have been discovered!

STANTON MOTEL
Located on Highway 66 at Stanton, Mo.

(P92) STANTON MOTEL (c.1949). The "Nearest Motel to Meramec Caverns," the Stanton advertised "Air-conditioned, Central Heat, Tubs or Showers. Low Rates." Even "Winter Rates." Someone stayed in cabin #5 ("X").

(P93) CAVERN CITY COURT (1939). Originally a 4-cabin complex with a campground, cafe, concrete block wash house and pump house (both still standing). In 1949 a filling station and garage were added. The cafe pictured is now the present office, with a new restaurant adjoining. (This may be one of the first "pump jockeys"!)

"MARTHA JANE FARM" 'AUTO COURT DELUXE' 'WONDER PLACE IN THE OZARKS"
1 MI. E. OF SULLIVAN, MO.   ON HI 66   62 MI. S-W FROM ST. LOUIS, MO.

(P94) MARTHA JANE FARM AUTO COURT. Preston Pyser, a retired corncob pipe salesman from Washington, Missouri, and his wife Martha Jane, lived on their farm in the 2-story house with a circle drive around it. Eventually four cabins were added ($1 - $5 in 1939). Quite a promoter, Preston once lured motorists by advertising "Stop & See the Bats," only to reveal a barrel full of baseball bats! (At the top of the drive is cabin #1.) The rock entrance wall (L) remains.

"MARTHA JANE FARM" 'AUTO COURT DELUXE' 'WONDER PLACE IN THE OZARKS''
1 MI. E. OF SULLIVAN, MO.   ON HI 66   62 MI. S-W FROM ST. LOUIS, MO.

(P95)   MARTHA JANE FARM AUTO COURT.   "Sleep in safety and comfort without extravagance." Each heated cabin came with hot and cold water, shower, toilet. The court was renamed Deluxe Cabins by new owner Edna Wagner and her son Gene in 1946. It stayed open until 1970. The house and a couple of cabins still stand. (Photo shows cabin # 1)

(P96) THE WHITE SWAN RESTAURANT. For years the restaurant also served as the Greyhound Bus depot. Later it became the White Swan Tavern, then was razed in 1989.

(P97) SULLMO HOTEL & CABINS. A private residence converted into a "hotel" in the early 1930s, a 1935 Conoco travel directory listed the hotel and cottages as renting for $1.50 a night. The Sullmo advertised the rooms as being "equipped with Simmons beds and inner spring mattresses, private showers and lavatories. Drinking water approved by the Mo. State Board of Health." The kitchen offered chicken, steak & country ham. "You have tried the rest, now try the best."

(P98) CAMPBELL CHEVROLET. Shown in the background next to Juergens Station (Henry Juergens is on the left), the car dealership was built as a garage (1926-1950) by G.E. Campbell, became a skating rink/restaurant, then a garage again. Currently it is the Chamber of Commerce building.

(P99) JUERGENS STATION. This view is to the east, looking past the station built by Henry Juergens in the early 1930s (the first in Sullivan). There is now an insurance company on the site.

SHAMROCK COURT
U. S. Hwy. 66
Sullivan, Missouri

(P100) SHAMROCK COURT (1945). This native stone court featured "Big, airy, quiet, homelike cabins, each with modern bath. Dining room service. Hollywood Beds." Mr. & Mrs. F.E. Dobbs were owners when this card was mailed in 1950.

(P101) FRIESENHAM DAIRY FARM. Leo Friesenham finished this rockwork around 1928 on his dairy farm that also included his rock silo, that became a Route 66 landmark.

(P102) ROEDEMEIER GARAGE. Built by the Souders Bros. (1925), the garage was purchased by Oscar Roedemeier in 1929, offering Shell, then Standard gas, and a restaurant that became a Greyhound bus stop.

(P103) BOURBON TOWER. The famous "Bourbon" tower (on the north side of I-44) was built in 1925 and has been the subject of various news articles across the country.

(P104) TINERS PLACE. Built in 1929 by Harry & Mae Tiner. The three cabins in back (with community toilets) rented for $1 to $2.50 in 1938. The house on the right was later gutted and became a "Dine & Dance" joint, featuring the "Merry Makers" with the Reiner boys. From 1944 to 1983 it was operated as Jim's Service Station (truck stop/cafe) by owner Jim McIntosh.

(P105) MARGE & BERNIE. Bernard Suttmueller built this filling station and lunch room in 1931, just after US 66 was paved here. Named for his two daughters who operated the gas hand pumps, the station also had 5-, 10-, & 25-cent slot machines. Bernard is pictured on the left with his friend W.C. (Bud) Rohrer in 1932.

(P106) MARGE & BERNIE. Bernard added three tourist cabins in 1935 that rented for $3 - $5 a night. His daughter Bernie and her husband Art Whitworth bought the property in 1946, running it until 1952, when Route 66 was relocated. That's Art (who had driven for Brasher Freight) in front of the then-Sinclair station. In 1933, a plate lunch of T-bone steak, fries, vegetable and coffee sold for 25 cents! (Overhead cost of the T-bone: 7 cents!)

(P107) BOURBON LODGE. Built by Alex & Edith Mortenson in 1932, the lodge had three cabins (one renting for 50 cents a night!). A breakfast of bacon, eggs, toast and coffee cost 25 cents. A fourth cabin was added, along with a Phillips 66 station. The cabins, with private toilets and showers, rented for $1 - $1.50 in 1939. The station building and a couple of the cabins (in the trees) still stand.

(P108) HI HILL. Alex & Edith Mortenson (Bourbon Lodge) moved west to the top of the hill and built the Hi Hill cabins and station. Jewell & Lillian Heitman then owned the enterprise from 1947 to 1955. The three single cabins rented for $3; the double for $5. The house/station, one cabin, and the water tower remain.

Rock of Ages, Onondaga Cave

(P109) ONONDAGA CAVE. Opened by Lester Dill (Meramec Caverns), Onondaga Cave (discovered by Daniel Boone) is Missouri's largest and billed as "America's most beautiful." This postcard shows Deborah Warning Ransom (R) and Sylvia Ryan (at the time, waitresses in the restaurant) on the Rock of Ages, a giant column 50 feet high. A registered national landmark, "Onondaga" translates from the Indian to "Spirit of the Mountain."

(P110) HOFFLIN STORE. This store was located at the old Jct. of the Springfield Road (US66) and the road leading to Argo to the north. Built prior to 1917, the store was purchased by Roy (pictured) & Lizzie Libhart in 1921, who operated it until the late 1940s. Hofflin store also had Red Crown Gasoline pumps, "For Power Mileage." (The store stayed open into the 1950s when highway expansion took its toll.)

(P111) LAZY Y CAMP. Built in the late 1920s, the Lazy Y is pictured in the mid-1930s when operated by Harry Comfort. The camp (with cafe, Phillips 66 pumps, and eight cabins - $1/night) was located at the "Y" merger of Route 66 and the old Springfield Road that paralleled the railroad. The cafe, run by the entire family, offered chicken, ham, or roast beef dinners with mashed potatoes and gravy, vegetable, hot biscuits, and dessert for 50 cents! (Some cabins remain)

(P112) PAUL'S CAFE. Originally called the Wagon Wheel Annex (1944), then Paul's Cafe (for owner Paul Killeen) and Cooke Service Station, it was later changed to Annex Cafe. This Phillips 66 station/cafe remained in operation until I-44 was completed (1965).

RED HORSE CABINS,
Cuba, Mo.,

East side of town, Highway 66.

(P113) RED HORSE CABINS (c.1938). "Sleep in safety and comfort at reasonable prices." (The six cottages with private toilet and showers were $1.50 - $2.50 a night in 1939) The cafe and garage were open 24 hours and the station had Mobilgas. "We service your car while you sleep." Later a truck stop was opened here ("the largest between St. Louis and Springfield"), but was destroyed by a spectacular fire that even closed down Route 66 (1953).

WAGON WHEEL
MOTEL
CUBA, MO.

Located East Side of Town on Highway U. S. 66

(P114) WAGON WHEEL MOTEL. This classic Route 66 motel began as the Wagon Wheel Cabins (1934). "Sleep in safety and comfort without extravagance." Built of "Colorful Ozark Stone," the nine cottages with private tub or shower bath grew to 14 in 1946. "Popular priced dining room, famous for the food in connection." A 1939 edition of a AAA travel guide proclaimed the Wagon Wheel "one of the best in the state!"

(P115) **HOTEL CUBA** (c.1915). This hotel property faced the old Springfield Road (MO 14) and Frisco tracks. Another entrance was built in back to accommodate the new Route 66. "Steam Heated and Air Cooled Rooms. Phone No. 9." A 1946 AAA guide stated the hotel, with its 20 rooms (eight with baths), was the "best available."

(P116) **MIDWAY.** "Always Open," the Midway was a restaurant and hotel with a "storied" history. From 1934, the new owner Allyne Earls kept the doors open 24 hours a day for 38 years. These 1952 Chevys were part of the Earls Cab fleet.

(P117) BARNETT MOTOR CO. This Ford Sales and Service dealership was built by A.J. Barnett in the 1920s, supplying Red Crown gasoline. Shown in 1930, A.J. is second from the right (next to the "Missouri US 66" sign), with his son William James fourth to the right of the Mobiloil display stand.

(P118) PEOPLES BANK. Founded in 1906 with "Capital & Surplus $22,000.00." A. J. Barnett became president, after being the first teller. The bank moved from this location in 1959 to its present location. The view is looking west along what became Route 66.

(P119) B&M CAFE. Built around 1930 (just after Route 66 was paved) by Art Eads and called Eads Cafe. In 1939, Bill Weise purchased the property and renamed it B&M Cafe (for Bill and Mary, his stepdaughter). In the 1950s, it served as the Greyhound and MK&O Agency, providing "Good Food - Novelties."

(P120) GRAPE STAND. One of many grape stands along Old 66 (I-44 south outer road) near Rosati now being threatened closure due to the amount of traffic parking on the shoulder of the interstate to make purchases. This stand's motto was "Have Grapes Will Sale."

(P121) ST. JAMES INN (c.1925). Although the main building faced the old Springfield Road and the railroad, the St. James Inn's five cabins (on a horseshoe drive in back) were accessible from Route 66. Later, a swimming pool was added in the middle of the "horseshoe." The Inn offered "rest rooms, furnished cottages, camp grounds, baths, hot and cold lunches, barbeque, and all-nite auto service" in the Pierce Pennant Oil Station. (The cabins and pool are gone.)

(P122) ATLASTA SERVICE STATION (1929). The Atlasta had a coffee shop, lunch counter, office and station downstairs in the main building, a banquet room/dancehall upstairs, a tire shop to the west (once with two large display windows), and cabins in back. The cafe offered "Dinners" and "Short Orders." The Atlasta was destroyed by fire in 1964, with only the tire shop being "spared." Love the bus!

(P123) DELANO OIL SERVICE STATION (1938). This photo shows operator Floyd Ballance filling up a Chevy at the station/cafe. The station originally used Tydol, then DX gasoline, offering a "Truck Discount." (Note the expansion underway to the left of the building.) Delano Oil is still based in St. James.

ROSE CAFE, ST. JAMES, MO.

(P124) ROSE CAFE (1929). Built for Jesse F. Rose, this onetime cafe/bus stop (also called Commercial Cafe) has been operated by John Bullock since 1950 as Johnnie's Bar and Indian relic "museum."

(P125) ROCK HAVEN. Frank and Ruth Waring bought the property in 1950 and built a restaurant and a new Standard station adjacent to the Rock Haven Cabins. The restaurant/station became a tavern/nightclub in the 1970s, and is now a private residence.

(P126) ROCK HAVEN CABINS. These six "modern" sandstone slab "giraffe rock" cabins, built just after Route 66 opened (c.1928), offered hot and cold showers in a community wash house, along with a filling station. Only one cabin remains; the others were torn down in 1988.

DILLON COURT--HWY. 66, 5 MI. EAST OF ROLLA, MO.

(P127) DILLON COURT. Built in the early 1940s, and named for the Dillon school district, the court was originally five unconnected cabins. Josephine & Clarence Nowak later changed the name to Country Aire, building a single roof connecting all the units. With its many variety of flowers and fruit trees, the park-like atmosphere for their campground was once considered a "place of beauty."

(P128) THRIFTY INN (early 1950s) **and DELANO THRIFTY SERVICE** (1940). The Thrifty Inn restaurant (now the nostalgia gift shop) has been connected to the service station (office) of Route 66 Motors, owned and operated by Wayne & Pat Bales.

94

RAMEYS CAFE, MILE EAST OF ROLLA, MO., ON U S 66

(P129) RAMEY'S CAFE. Built in the late 1930s as a truck stop/restaurant featuring "Home Cooked Food," after the war it became a popular hamburger joint for the local college students. Later turned into a tavern, Ramey's burned to the ground in 1970.

SINCLAIR PENNANT HOTELS
Columbia, Mo. (On U. S. Highway 40) — Rolla, Mo. (On U. S. Highways 66 and 63)

Complete hotel and restaurant accommodations of the highest type, designed especially for motorists. Service and facilities unexcelled in metropolitan areas.

(P130) SINCLAIR PENNANT HOTEL (1928). This once grandiose hotel was built by Pierce Petroleum to be "the answer to America's demand for comfort and convenience on the highway...far ahead of anything else by the roadside." (In 1935 the 40 rooms rented for $4 up.) It was soon taken over by Sinclair, then remodeled by its then-owner into Carney Manor (1963); later razed to make way for the new Drury Inn.

(P131) VIEW OF 66 - US 66/63. This 1959 view is to the northeast, with US 63 (old 2-lane 66) crossing over 4-lane New 66 toward the Pennant Hotel. To travel east on New 66, you would veer right, then left, then right onto the 4-lane. According to the sign, "To Go West Go Over Bridge And Make Two Right Turns."

(P132) PENNANT TAVERN (1928). "Located in or near the Ozark Mountain country," this restaurant and service station was down the hill from its "sister" Pennant Hotel.

(P133) **PENNANT CAFE.** Originally the Pennant Tavern, modifications were made to provide food and hotel accommodations. Renamed Pennant Cafe and Hotel Martin by owners/operators Mr. & Mrs. R.W. Martin, it partly burned in the 1953, later entirely razed.

(P134) **COLONIAL VILLAGE HOTEL** (1938). This hotel, with cabins in back, had a restaurant "Famous for Fine Food." A 1935 Shell directory listed the 24 rooms as renting for $1 - $1.75. A 1946 AAA guide called the $3 - $4 rooms "attractive." Owned and operated as Frederick's from 1963 to 1976 by Fred & Vernelle Gasser (previous owners of Vernelle's Motel west of town).

TRAV-L-ODGE
ROLLA, MISSOURI

(P135) TRAV-L-ODGE TOURIST COURT & STEAKHOUSE. These cabins and steakhouse ("conveniently located on Hwy 66 at Rolla, the Gateway to the Ozarks"), featured "delicious Broiled Steaks and Sea Foods. Modern, steam-heated units." The Pennant Hotel can be seen on the hill at right.

AND
SHOWER BATHS.
•
TELEPHONES
•
RADIOS
•
STEAM
HEAT.

INTERIOR OF COTTAGE

LOBBY OF HOTEL

SCHUMAN'S TOURIST CITY, ROLLA, MISSOURI, ON U. S. 66 AND 63.

(P136) SCHUMAN'S TOURIST CITY (Late 1920s). With a service station and cafe, and, in the late 1930s, accommodations for 100 guests, this "city" had "all the facilities of a fine hotel. Grounds are patrolled all night by watchman who carries watchclock which he punches at stations in all parts of the court and all floors of hotel." The cottages in front were razed with the widening of US 66, and a second story was added to the "new" units in back. (See photo P137)

(P137) AERIAL VIEW OF 66 - ROLLA. North, overlooking US 66/63 toward the newly opened (1954) 4-lane 66. At top is Schuman's Tourist City. To the left is the old Bell Garage (c.1927), built by Robert Bell, that became a cafe in the 1930s (and the original Greyhound and MK&O depot). Closed in the early 1950s, it is now a flea market. At center, the "new" Greyhound depot (1947 - since razed), built to compete with the Pickwick Bus Line depot at the nearby Pennant Cafe.

(P138) VIEW OF 66 - ROLLA. This view is looking east from Jct. Route 66 & Pine. On the left, Schuman's Tourist City, and on the right is the old Bell Cafe/Greyhound depot.

"New and Modern"

On U. S. Highway 66 and 63. Phelps Oil Company, Rolla, Missouri

(P139) PHELPS MODERN COTTAGES (c.1934). Built by the Phelps Oil Co., they advertised "Sleep where sleeping is safe. 16 modern, steam-heated and air-conditioned fireproof cottages. Tile tub and shower baths, radios. Free garages, locked. Popular price cafe, famous for good foods. We service your car while you sleep. Phone, Mail, and Western Union service." With porter and maid service (and laundry facilities), this was "one of the finest auto courts in the Ozarks."

(P140) ROLLA POST OFFICE. Built in 1921, this structure now houses the Rolla Free Public Library.

(P141) ROLLAMO THEATRE. This old theatre has been remodeled into the present Boatmen's Bank.

HOTEL EDWIN LONG — ROLLA, MO.

(P142) HOTEL EDWIN LONG (1931). Built by M.E. Gilloiz and named for Senator Edwin Long, a prominent local civic leader and businessman who had died in 1928. Opened for business on March 12, 1931, the hotel served as headquarters for the celebration (March 15) of the completion (paving) of Route 66 across Missouri. The hotel had 65 rooms ($2 - $2.50), a coffee shop, meeting room, and offices of the National Bank of Rolla. (Phelps County Bank since 1960.)

(P143) MARTIN SPRING. Known as Sycamore Spring during the Civil War, in the late 1920s Bill and Emma Martin built a house/store (with gas pumps) on their farm (once the Bloom farm). They also operated a springhouse (rebuilt in the early 1950s after a car accident) where they sold milk and Emma's homemade butter. (The two "outhouses" still standing on the property were built by the WPA in 1940.) The kids in front of the store are Emma's niece and nephew (c.1940).

(P144) AARON'S OLD HOMESTEAD (1934). Run by the Aaron Bros., this station and cafe (still an Aaron residence) accepted Cities Service Charge Cards. The station is next to the old log cabin built by Joe Aaron in 1863.

(P145) AARON'S RADIATOR SERVICE (1937). The garage and radiator shop business at one time also was an Oldsmobile, Cadillac, and Jeep dealer. The sign out front read "This Is Aaron's Radiator Service." After becoming an Evinrude motor dealer, another sign boasted, "We Guarantee To Cool Your Motor." The business, still operating, moved into Rolla after Old 66 was bypassed by I-44.

(P146) TOTEM POLE TRADING POST. This was the second location (1967-1977) of the Totem Pole Trading Post (with Shell service). Now Gaunlet Paint, it faced 4-lane 66. (Old 2-lane 66 went behind.) The business moved into Rolla when I-44 access was eliminated.

(P147) MALONE'S SERVICE STATION. Built by the Hudson Oil Co. in 1941 and owned by Dan Malone since 1952, at one time there were 12 pumps, and a restaurant on the east side of the property (razed with new CO. T).

(P148) BENNETT'S CATFISH & CABINS (1943). Paul Bennett's first catfish cafe location was just a block west from Malone's station. The business was moved to Clementine (Basket Ridge) in 1952, after Route 66 relocation. The stone gateposts to the cabins still stand, as does the original cafe (by gas pumps), now a residence.

(P149) BENNETT'S CATFISH (Interior). Paul Bennett (in white shirt and tie) offered a bacon & eggs breakfast for 60 cents and a complete catfish dinner for $1!

(P150) TOWELL'S STORE & CABINS. This store/station, built by Ike & Edna Towell in 1928, was open 24-hours a day, seven days a week for close to 50 years. The three cottages with community toilets and shower (but with private cooking facilities) rented for $1 - $1.50 in 1938.

(P151) T&T CAFE (1952). Joe & Ruth Terrill Tabor (T&T) had a store (now a residence) next to the Towell Store, but after 66 was relocated to the north they built the T&T Cafe & Garage facing the 4-lane New 66. After losing access to I-44, the business closed. Since expanded, it is now I-44 Flea Market.

(P152) VERNELLE'S MOTEL. Originally a store/filling station, six cabins and a novelty shop (c.1938) owned by E.P. Gasser and called Gasser Tourist Court. Fred & Vernelle Gasser bought the property from his uncle in 1952 and built a restaurant and motel. The restaurant was razed (and the other buildings relocated) in 1957 to accommodate the new outer road for US 66 expansion. The Gassers sold, moved to Rolla, and later operated the old Colonial Village Hotel.

(P153) VIEW OF 66 - ARLINGTON AREA. The view in this photo (1965) is to the west toward the hill going down to Arlington (left lanes are original 66) showing the Totem Pole Trading Post (bottom left), the Ozark Trading Post (Novelty House), the OK Diner (once Country Village), the Beacon Hill Motel (top right), and (lower right) the Jones family residence (owners of the Totem Pole). The businesses on the left were razed with construction of the I-44 outer road.

(P154) TOTEM POLE TOURIST CAMP (1933-1961). This "complex" grew to include the souvenir shop, a Standard (later Shell) station (still standing), six log cabins, the family residence, and even a coin-operated laundry! After the realignment of Route 66 in 1953, the cabins were moved to the north (three still stand next to the remodeled residence).

(P155) TOTEM POLE TRADING POST (1961-1967). A few years after this expansion, the business relocated further east, toward Rolla. Visible to the far right of the photo is part of the original log gas station, all that remains on this site.

(P156) BEACON HILL MOTEL (c.1935). Named for its airline beacon atop a tower, the Beacon Hill Tourist Camp was comprised of nine unheated cabins, with community toilets available. A filling station and restaurant were added later (both razed for New 4-lane 66 - 1953). The cabins were then connected and a new restaurant built (shown). After access was lost to I-44 the business closed.

Why'd They Name It That?

(See page 261)

(P157) STONYDELL (1932). Stonydell was a public resort built by George Prewett that included a large swimming pool, restaurant, service station, Trailways bus stop and (in 1939) ten cabins ($1 - $2 a night). It offered dancing, tennis, boating, fishing, and even a Justice of the Peace! Stonydell was so popular with locals and Route 66 travelers that many days highway patrolmen had to direct traffic! (Historically, in the 1830s part of the Cherokee Indians camped here on their Trail of Tears odyssey.) Fred Widener owned the property from 1954 to 1967, when the dual lanes were added to US 66. The highway department purchased the land, and all on the south side of original US 66 was razed.

(P158) VIEW OF 66 - ARLINGTON AREA. This view (September, 1953) is looking east toward Arlington and the Little Piney River. The Missouri Highway Department crew is finishing work on the new eastbound lanes of US 66 (now the westbound lanes of I-44). (Note the Viking truck climbing the original 2-lane 66, now the outer road of I-44.)

(P159) PECAN JOE'S. This Texas chain operation became locally owned by Vic Lomax in the mid-60s. Famous for their pecan candy, they were into Ozark souvenirs as well. "Headquarters for gifts of the Ozarks and Pecan Joe's famous candies." Razed in 1967, after being bypassed.

(P160) POWELLVILLE. Built in the early 1930s by the Powell brothers, who had one of the largest trucking companies operating on Route 66. This picture (c.1932) shows the original layout of Powellville, consisting of a 24-hour service station/restaurant/store, and 10 cabins.

(P161) POWELLVILLE. Later a new "rocked" Powellville office was built, along with the "rocking" of the 10 cabins (listed in a 1938 Shell guide as being with private toilets and showers for $1.50 - $2.50 a night). "Accommodations for Large Parties." After 4-lane 66 bypassed this stretch of Old 66 (1967), the property was purchased by the Forestry Department and razed.

(P162) BENNETT'S CATFISH CAFE. Built by Venita Roberts in 1948 as a private residence, this "giraffe rock" building later housed the relocated Bennett's Catfish Cafe (1952) until I-44 cut off direct access (1967). A connecting motel and service station were destroyed by fire in 1970.

(P163) HILLBILLY STORE. Built by Sterling Wells' father with the new 4-lane 66 construction (c.1943). (The Wells family's first store had been on old 2-lane 66 in Hooker.) This store, across from the "entrance" to Hooker, was closed after I-44 bypassed it (1981).

(P164) HOOKER CHURCH & CEMETERY. Still standing, both date to the early 1900s.

(P165) FANCHER STORE. This store/post office (with Red Crown gasoline) once stood on Old 2-lane 66 near the present location of I-44 (to the north).

(P166) VIEW OF 66 - HOOKER CUT. This view is looking west from the town of Hooker toward the Hooker Cut in the late 1940s.

Big Cut on U. S. Highway 66 at Hooker,
between Lebanon and Rolla, Missouri,
in the Beautiful Ozarks

(P167) HOOKER CUT (1942). At one time, this was the deepest highway rock cut in America. (The view on the postcard is to the west.)

(P168) VIEW OF 66 - HOOKER CUT. Looking east along the recently paved New 66 toward Hooker from above the Hooker Cut. At the top left of the photo can be seen the bypassed 2-lane Old 66 curving through town.

New U. S. Highway 66 Crossing Big Piney River between Rolla and Waynesville, Mo.   *BL 56*

(P169) VIEW OF 66 - BIG PINEY. This view from the Jct. of 4-lane New 66 and 2-lane Old 66 is to the west towards the bridge (1942) crossing the Big Piney River.

(P170) DALE'S SPORTING GOODS (1950). Dale's (once with a liquor store/grocery and Phillips 66 station) was a gathering place for area sportsmen. Built by Dale Hooker (of the local Hooker family), the business was sold in 1969, and is now owned by Bruce & Thelma Debo, whose **Roubidoux Woodworkers** produces wooden fishing lures, spoons, and mechanical puzzles.

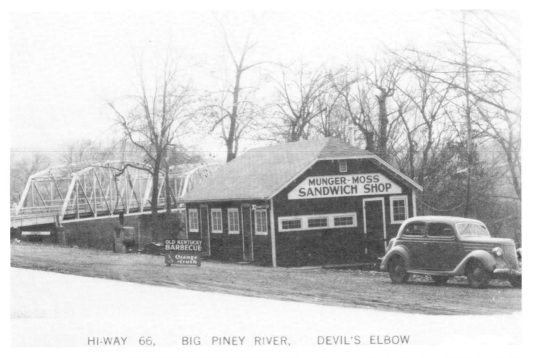

HI-WAY 66, BIG PINEY RIVER, DEVIL'S ELBOW

(P171) MUNGER-MOSS SANDWICH SHOP. This cafe was built in the late 1930s by Nelle Munger and Emmett Moss on a site just before the bridge crossing the Big Piney River. They offered "Old Kentucky Barbeque" and "Orange Crush."

BIG PINEY RIVER,   DEVIL'S ELBOW   HIGHWAY 66

(P172) MUNGER-MOSS SANDWICH SHOP. After adding a gift shop and residence, Nelle & Emmett Moss offered barbeque chicken, ribs, beef, pork and ham, along with Hyde Park beer. Also, "Good Coffee - Milk - Pie," and "Special Ho Made Ice Cream."

(P173) ELBOW INN. After the Munger-Moss relocated to Lebanon, MO (1946), Paul & Nadine Thompson reopened under the new name, operating into the 1960s. Ever the "card," Paul once placed two glasses of water in front of new customers from Massachusetts, saying to local Bruce Debo, "Look Debo, the river cleared up!" (The couple cleared out!)

118

(P174) DEVILS ELBOW CAFE. Built by Dwight Rench (c.1932), the cafe and Conoco station was affiliated with Cedar Lodge (that had 10 cabins with private cooking facilities). This view shows the old Big Piney Bridge and the bluffs along the river. (The original building burned in the late 1970s.)

Devil's Elbow, Scenic Spot on U. S. Highway 66

(P175) DEVILS ELBOW CAFE. The cafe was "where the main street of America (U.S. Hwy. 66) winds its way through one of the most scenic areas in the Ozark region." This was the Devils Elbow post office from 1933-1941.

(P176) MILLER'S MARKET. This store with Conoco gas pumps was built by Dorothy & Atholl (Jiggs) Miller in 1954, next door to his father-in-law's store, and has been the post office since. The store was bought by Terry & Marilyn Allman (the current postmaster) in 1982. (That's Jiggs in the window.)

(P177) MC COYS STORE & CAMP. Built by Charles McCoy in 1941 as a store with sleeping rooms upstairs (shown here in 1948); cabins were added later. (Some remain.) The post office was moved here in 1941, staying until 1954 when his son-in-law Jiggs Miller moved it next door.

THE
MISSOURI
US
66
TOUR BOOK

MAP SECTION

ST. LOUIS AREA

Listed on the National Register of Historic Places

- **Gateway Arch** (1965) commemorating St. Louis as the Gateway to the West, is the country's tallest man-made monument (630 ft.). Tram to top, visitor center, museum. (314) 982-1410.

- **Eads Bridge** (1874) spans the Mississippi River. An engineering marvel, it's the world's first steel-truss bridge.

- **Laclede's Landing**, site of the city's original settlement, is a renovated district of cobblestone streets with shops, restaurants, offices and condos. Next to Eads Bridge.

- **Anheuser Busch Brewery**, the world's largest, offers free tours of the Clydesdale stables (1885), Brewhouse (1892), etc. Complimentary samples available.

- **Union Station** (1894) (18th & Market) at one time the biggest and busiest railroad station in the world. Now a retail shopping mall.

- **Forest Park**. Site of the 1904 Louisiana Purchase Exposition (St. Louis World's Fair) that gave us ice cream cones, hot dogs and iced tea. The 1300 acres include the Art Museum (1904), Jewel Box greenhouse (1936), the Muny Opera, the nation's oldest (1919) and largest outdoor stage theater (12,000 seats-1400 free), and the St. Louis Zoo with its famous Birdhouse (1904).

- St. Louis Visitor Bureau: (800) 888-3861.

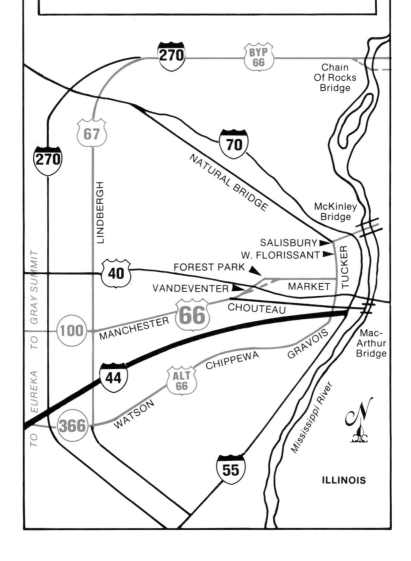

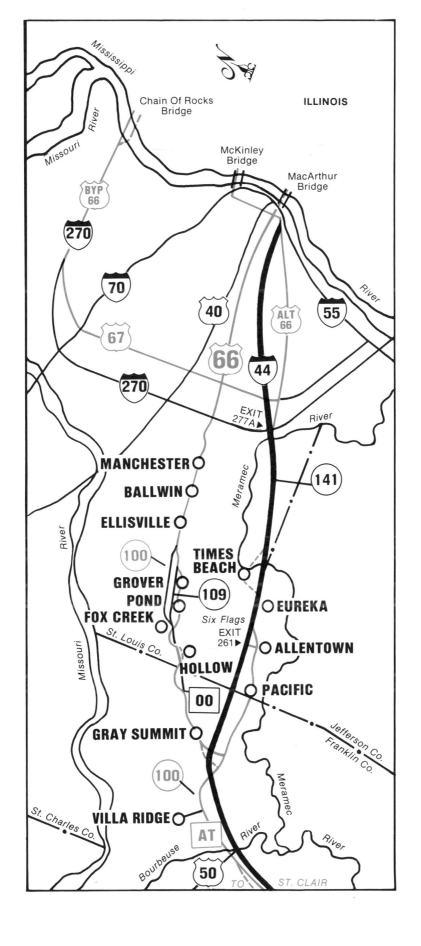

123

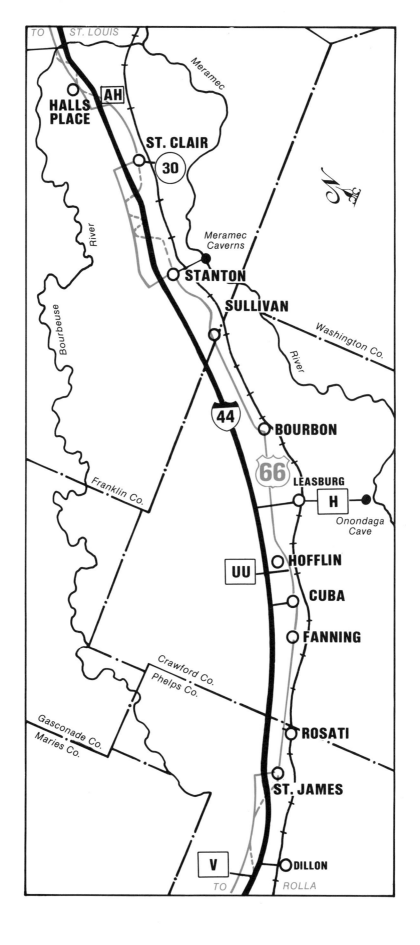

TO ST. LOUIS

Meramec

HALLS PLACE

AH

ST. CLAIR
30

River

Meramec Caverns

Bourbeuse

STANTON

SULLIVAN

Washington Co.

River

44

BOURBON

Franklin Co.

66
LEASBURG
H
Onondaga Cave

UU
HOFFLIN

CUBA

FANNING

Crawford Co.
Phelps Co.

Gasconade Co.
Maries Co.

ROSATI

ST. JAMES

V
DILLON

TO ROLLA

124

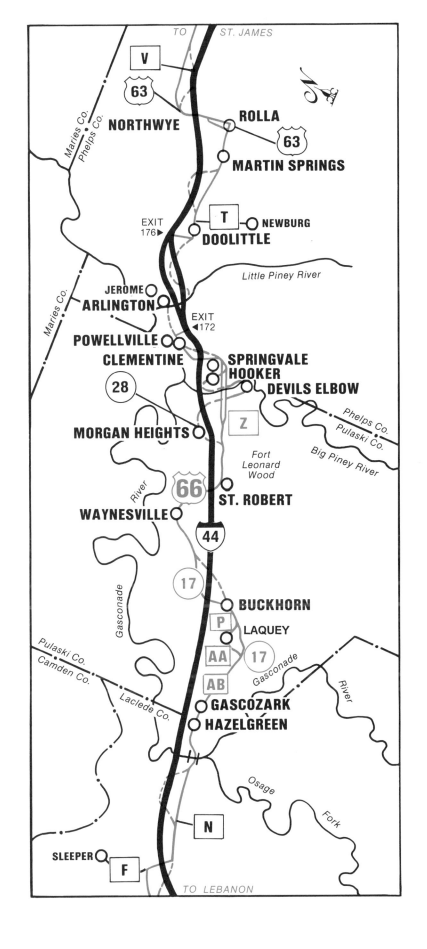

TO ST. JAMES

V

63

NORTHWYE

ROLLA

63

MARTIN SPRINGS

Maries Co.
Phelps Co.

EXIT 176 ▶

T

NEWBURG

DOOLITTLE

Little Piney River

Maries Co.

JEROME
ARLINGTON

EXIT ◀172

POWELLVILLE

CLEMENTINE

SPRINGVALE
HOOKER

DEVILS ELBOW

28

Phelps Co.
Pulaski Co.

MORGAN HEIGHTS

Z

Fort
Leonard
Wood

Big Piney River

River

66

ST. ROBERT

WAYNESVILLE

44

Gasconade

17

BUCKHORN

P

LAQUEY

Pulaski Co.
Camden Co.

AA

17

AB

Gasconade

River

Laclede Co.

GASCOZARK

HAZELGREEN

Osage

N

Fork

SLEEPER

F

TO LEBANON

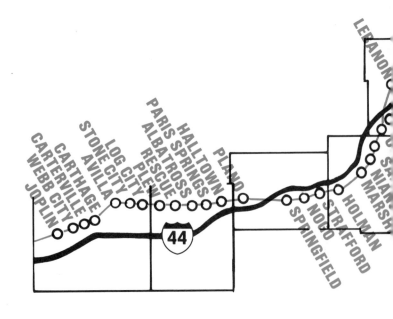

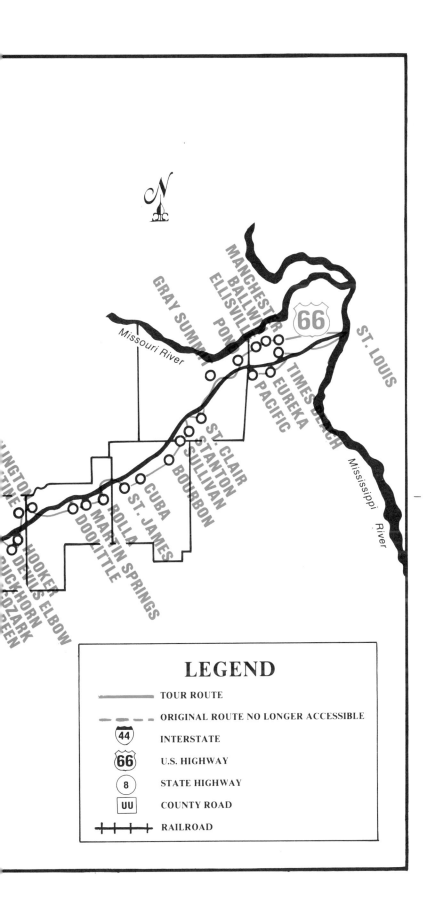

LEGEND

━━━━━ TOUR ROUTE

╌╌╌╌╌ ORIGINAL ROUTE NO LONGER ACCESSIBLE

(44) INTERSTATE

(66) U.S. HIGHWAY

(8) STATE HIGHWAY

[UU] COUNTY ROAD

┼┼┼┼ RAILROAD

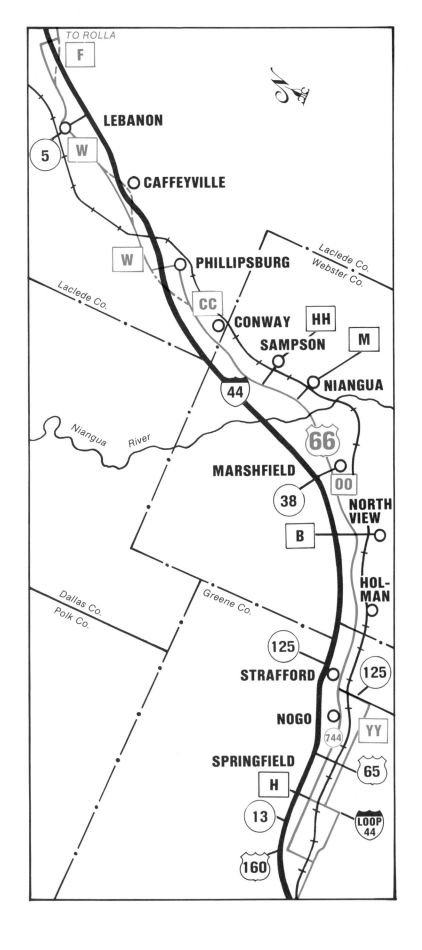

TO ROLLA
F

LEBANON

5 W

CAFFEYVILLE

W

PHILLIPSBURG

Laclede Co.
Webster Co.

CC

CONWAY HH

SAMPSON M

44 NIANGUA

Laclede Co.

Niangua River

66

MARSHFIELD 00

38 NORTH VIEW

B

HOL-MAN

Dallas Co.
Polk Co.

Greene Co.

125

STRAFFORD 125

NOGO YY
744

65

SPRINGFIELD

H

13 LOOP 44

160

SPRINGFIELD AREA

- **Wilson's Creek National Battlefield & Visitors Center.** Site of the first major Civil War battle west of the Mississippi (August, 1861) where over 2500 men lost their lives. Self-guided 5-mile auto tour, museum. (National Register of Historic Places.) (SW) Springfield. (417) 732-2662

- **Fantastic Caverns,** one of Missouri's largest, offers a 50 min. tram tour through the lighted cave that served as a speakeasy in the 1920s, and a country music theater in the 1960s and 1970s. (417) 833-2010.

- **Crystal Cave** is the second oldest commercial cavern in Missouri (opened 1893). Originally inhabited by the Osage Indian; tours pass some of their gravesites. (417) 833-9599.

- **Bass Pro Shops Outdoor World**, in south Springfield, is the world's largest sporting goods store, featuring a 4-story indoor waterfall, live alligators, massive aquariums, and a restaurant. (800) 227-7776.

- **Exotic Animal Paradise**, America's greatest drive-thru animal park. View over 3,000 exotic birds and rare animals from your car. On old Route 66 east of town. Open all year. (417) 468-2016.

- **Branson**. 35 miles south of Springfield, this mecca of live country music shows is situated on Lake Taneycomo, next to Table Rock Lake. This area provided the setting for Harold Bell Wright's best-selling novel *The Shepherd of the Hills.*

- Nearby Branson is **Silver Dollar City**, a combination Ozark settlement (demonstrating traditional crafts) and an old-time theme park. (417) 338-8100.

- Springfield Visitors Bureau: (800) 678-8766.

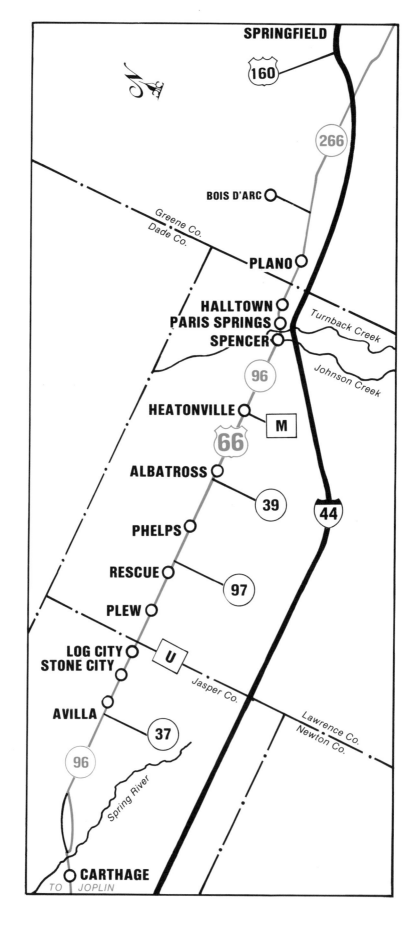

SPRINGFIELD

160

266

BOIS D'ARC

Greene Co.
Dade Co.

PLANO

HALLTOWN
PARIS SPRINGS
SPENCER

Turnback Creek

Johnson Creek

96

HEATONVILLE

M

66

ALBATROSS

39

44

PHELPS

RESCUE

97

PLEW

LOG CITY
STONE CITY

U

Jasper Co.

AVILLA

Lawrence Co.
Newton Co.

37

96

Spring River

CARTHAGE

TO JOPLIN

130

CARTHAGE-JOPLIN AREA

- **Thomas Hart Benton Mural & Exhibit** in Joplin. Only autobiographical mural by this Missouri artist. 1-800-657-2534. Also, the last mural by Benton, in the Joplin Municipal Building.

- **Precious Moments Chapel**, in 17-acre center, created by artist Samuel Butcher, highlighted by his famous porcelain figurines, SW of Carthage. 1-800-543-7975.

- **Red Oak II**, an early American community built and restored by Lowell Davis, Missouri sculptor and painter. 417-358-9018.

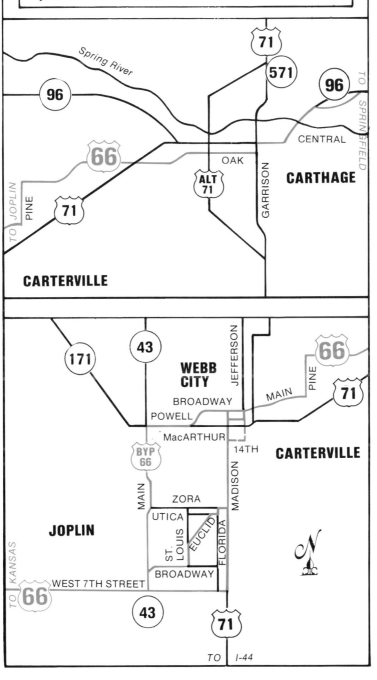

THE

MISSOURI
U S
66

TOUR BOOK

(P178) GRAHAM'S RESORT. This country general store was purchased in 1925 by Walter Graham, who added a cafe, filling station, and ten cabins ($1.25 - $3 in 1936) along the bend of the Big Piney River. The store/resort (Devils Elbow's first post office, 1927-1933) became so popular that cabins rented "by appointment only." Now called River Park, six cabins are still available.

(P179) VIEW OF 66 - DEVILS ELBOW. This view is of a stretch of original US 66 west of Devils Elbow, looking east. Pictured is the original rock retaining wall next to a scenic overlook of the Big Piney River valley, and the "half-curbs" intended to keep cars on the road (but often as not would flip them over). Among the reduced traffic flow today are these guinea fowl!

(P180) **DEVILS ELBOW MOTEL.** Built around 1950 and run by the McClary family, the motel was advertised as "New - Clean - Modern - Heated - Air Conditioned." After Interstate 44 bypassed this section (1981), the motel was used as rental property.

(P181) **VIEW OF 66 - MORGAN HEIGHTS.** Pictured is a secluded "unused" section of original Old 66 that was cut off when the 4-lane New 66 was completed in the 1940s. Great to wander on!

(P182) SCOTT GARAGE. Built by Dorsey Scott (c.1928) to service traffic at the Jct. of Old Route 66 & then-MO 17 (now Missouri Ave-CO. Y). With the building of Fort Wood the business installed a rather "elaborate" rock front and expanded to include a drug store and offered food, drinks & "Dime-A-Dance." Even strung some lights! It was torn down with the coming of I-44.

RANCH MOTEL — Route 2 — Waynesville, Missouri

(P183) RANCH MOTEL. Built in the early 1940s, this motel was "2 Miles East of Town on '66' " (Waynesville). Since "rocked," it is still operating as a motel.

(P184) OAKWOOD VILLAGE (c.1940). Neil "Doc" Williams (an old buddy of then-Senator Harry Truman) bought property and built this court after he somehow learned of the impending construction of nearby Fort Leonard Wood. The "village" consisted of a store/cafe, station/office, and "Modern Cottages," equipped with hot-water heat. All was razed with the building of I-44.

(P185) PULASKI COUNTY COURTHOUSE (1903). On the National Register of Historic Places, the courthouse now houses the county history museum.

(P186) VICTORY TAVERN/WAYNESVILLE CAFE. This building, housing Victory Liquor, Victory Tavern, and Waynesville Cafe, was built by George "The Greek" Morris in 1942 (who had changed his name after immigration to America). The businesses have been continuously run since by members of his family.

(P187) BELL HOTEL. Robert A. Bell (a local attorney) expanded his home into a hotel in anticipation of the new highway. Operated by the Bell family from 1925 to 1937, the hotel advertised "Every Facility for the Traveler's Pleasure. Old Southern Hospitality." Now a funeral home; the floral shop in front was Bell's Sinclair filling station (1930).

137

(P188) D&D MARKET. Originally Upton Market (1941), it became D&D (Deutschman & Deutschman) in 1947. It had a cafe and Mobil (then Standard) gas pumps, cabins to the side, and feed store in back. The market is now a crafts shop; the feed store still stands; the cabins are gone.

(P189) AERIAL VIEW OF 66 - BUCKHORN. This view is looking north past the D&D Market, showing their cabins to the left and the feed store in back. (New 4-lane 66/I-44, now runs directly through the open field behind the D&D feed store.)

(P190) PLEASANT GROVE CABINS (c.1932). In 1935 the five cottages (with private cooking facilities) rented for $1 - $1.50. This view (1943) is when Rudy & Clara Schuermann owned the property. In 1948 it was sold to the Bell family who changed the name to Bell Haven Court. The Sinclair pumps were later taken out and the drive-under canopy enclosed.

(P191) NORMANDY (1932). The Normandy was a hotel, gas station and restaurant that later became a rather bawdy roadhouse. After the nearby quarry opened, the Normandy shut down and was razed (c.1978 - Local volunteer firemen would periodically set fire to the building to practice extinguishing the blaze. One time the fire got out of control, and the structure was finally destroyed!)

(P192) HILLCREST GROCERIES & STATION (1932). Built by Vern Smith and his dad Guy of native rock, the station used KanOTex gas. The store is now Vern's residence.

CENTRAL MOTEL & SERVICE STATION--COMPLETELY MODERN--17 in. T.V. in ROOMS
12 MILES WEST OF WAYNESVILLE. MISSOURI--HIGHWAY 66

(P193) CENTRAL MOTEL & STATION. Ed Lentz took over this garage and station in 1951, built the adjoining motel, and settled in for some Route 66 business. Within five years the highway had bypassed this location. So Ed built the Oasis, a restaurant/station, north of the nearby new 4-lane 66. When that road was converted to I-44, access to his business was cutoff, and once again he had to relocate.

(P194) CALDWELL'S. This complex, owned by Dave Caldwell, originally consisted of four single cabins behind a 2-part building that housed a cafe (L) and store/station (R). Shown in December, 1939, gas was 12 cents a gallon! (Each unit was later expanded into a double, with shared bathroom. Three survive.)

(P195) CALDWELL'S. This is an interior view of the cafe, looking down the ten-stool counter toward the rear. (Note the souvenirs and novelties available.)

(P196) CALDWELL'S. After becoming Caldwell-Salsman, a larger cafe was added on the right of the structure, a stone service bay was added (still present), and the station was considered a "truck stop." (The section on the left was changed to a "bunkhouse" for the drivers.) The expanded building was then provided with a new stone front.

(P197) GASCOZARK CAFE. Built by Frank A. Jones, it was later operated by Rudy & Clara Schuermann, shown here in 1936 standing next to her nephew Norman Stoll (who supplied this photo) sitting on his mother's lap. Like most other early Route 66 businesses, the Gascozark sold handmade baskets. The Schuermanns later owned Pleasant Grove Cabins in Buckhorn.

"GASCOZARK" SERVICE STATION & CAFE
HI-WAYS 66   HAZLEGREEN MO.

(P198) GASCOZARK CAFE. After being "rocked" in 1939, the cafe/station became a Greyhound Bus depot in the 1940s, and the Spinning Wheel Tavern in the 50s.

(P199) WALKER BROS. RESORT. Brothers Elmer Lee & John Walker formed Walker Bros. Resort in 1916 across the road from Parsons Lodge. One of many local hunting and fishing resorts, the Walker consisted of a Sinclair station/store, dining room, six cabins ($2 a day with meals), and even a croquet & tennis court. Their rooftop sign boasted "Good Fishing, Boats & Guides, Meals, Rooms, Cabins," and "Tourist Welcome."

(P200) WALKER BROS. RESORT. This spacious dining room would serve customers breakfast and dinner, along with picnic baskets of fried chicken, potato salad, and homemade pie. Pictured are Alvia Mae Walker (L) and Mrs. Bud (Gladys) Chandler. "Call 168 R3" (three rings). The resort was sold to the Parsons family in the 1940s.

(P201) PARSONS LODGE. Will & Columbus Parsons bought a store here in the early 1900s and converted it and the family home into Parsons Lodge. It became a popular destination point for vacationers from St. Louis and surrounding areas, renting for $2 - $3 in 1935. It was razed in 1954 to "accommodate" US 66 expansion.

A Cozy Cottage at "Eden", Hazlegreen, Mo.

(P202) EDEN RESORT (c.1930). This was a popular "resort" for float trips and camping on the Gasconade River, used mostly by locals and vacationers. In 1935 there were 14 cabins, renting for $1.50 - $3.00. Only two cabins remain.

(P203) SUNRISE VIEW TOURIST COURT. Built in 1926 as six log cabins and a Standard gas station/restaurant, the Sunrise View was owned and operated by Lee & Marie Moore. The cabins (with community showers) rented for $1 - $1.50 a night in 1935 (summer season only). This 1929 photo shows Lee's son Herschel and his aunt and uncle, Ruth & Noel (Red) Moore.

(P204) THE HARBOR. Built around 1939 as a truck "port," the Harbor was a cafe/station with "Modern Cabins." Travelers sent this card with an indication ("Here we stayed") of where they had spent the night.

(P205) THE HARBOR (Interior). Pictured in 1954 is waitress Judy Lorance French, who "walked two miles to work in a starched uniform each day." The Harbor later became Brownie's Truck Stop, Andy's Midway (that later moved across the road to its present location), and then Geno's.

(P206) GENO'S. Geno Matella renamed his tavern Geno's, that according to locals served the "best pizza ever, bar none." This roadhouse and station, with "rooms" upstairs, burned in 1965. (The remaining building on site had been used as a gas station.)

(P207) RILEYS SNACK BAR (c.1940). Originally "Red Ball" gas station (railroad jargon for "Stop"), this store/station was owned and operated by Bud & Ruth Riley from 1947 to 1965. This picture shows the station in 1948 with Tydol "hand pumps." At left is their cabin for rent, still standing, as is one of their signs across the road.

RILEY'S SNACK BAR--9 MILES EAST OF LEBANON, MO.--U.S. 66
Gas--Beer--Souvenirs--Sandwiches

(P208) RILEYS SNACK BAR. Later converting to Sinclair, then Texaco gas in the 1950s, Rileys supplied fireworks, gas, beer, sandwiches, "sodee," and Ozark souvenirs, advertising "Coming or Going, This Is the Place to Stop." The Rileys first lived over the station, then moved to the house at right (site now occupied by a trailer). The station/store burned in 1965.

(P209) SATELLITE CAFE. Stating "Our desire is to make your trip a very pleasant one," the cafe offered "Fried Chicken, Steaks, Chops, Home Made pies. Carry Out Service. Free Picnic Area with Shady Tables." Their "Space Station" provided Phillips 66 products.

(P210) 4 ACRE COURT. Built in 1939 by Ray Coleman and Blackie Walters, the court was made up of "Family units and campground," along with the station/offfice/residence in front. The cottages are now rented as apartments.

(P211) VESTA COURT (c.1937). Advertised as "Beautiful Vesta Court," Clayton Lein owned and operated this 23-unit court. In 1957, Marie & Bill Williams bought the property, renaming it El Rancho Court. (The "Vesta Court" arch-sign over the entrance is presently at the B&D Truck Port on the west end of town, now labeled "Self Service Entrance." The foundations of the sign posts are still visible on the left.)

(P212) VESTA COURT (c.1937). The cafe/Texaco station was added in 1952. "Excellent Food. Open every day 6:30 am to 9:30 pm." (The foundation/ruins can still be seen next to the old road.) The cottages were razed after 4-lane New 66 bypassed this stretch of road in the middle 1960s.

(P213) SCOTTY'S TOURIST CITY. This grouping of cabins, cafe, and station/liquor store was built in the late 1940s by Dennis Scott. Presently, the old liquor store (now a garage) and one cabin are all that remain.

Munger Moss Motel
"on old Rt. 66" Lebanon, Missouri - Built in 1946

(P214) MUNGER-MOSS MOTOR COURT (MOTEL) (1946). Jessie & Pete Hudson (who had purchased the Munger-Moss Sandwich Shop in Devils Elbow before relocating in Lebanon) bought the Chicken Shanty Cafe (changing to Munger-Moss Barbeque), built a court of seven buildings with two units and garage each, and called the complex Munger-Moss Motor Court.

(P215) MUNGER-MOSS KEY. Like other courts, the Munger Moss was originally separate units with space between them. These were later covered for parking, and still later converted to additional units. To save the inconvenience of re-numbering all the units, these new cabins were given the "1/2" designation. Room "10-1/2" was for years the site of the biggest ongoing poker game (with "Clyde and the boys") in the county!

(P216) CLARK'S ROCK COURT (1930s). The court, "Open All Year," once had ten "Strictly Modern Cabins among the trees." The cafe was "Famous for Good Food." The station/truck stop offered "24 Hour Texaco Service." A few of the cabins remain.

(P217) ROCK COURT CAFE. By 1946 the cafe, although advertising "We Serve the Best of Everything-Chicken and Steak Dinners A Specialty," had become famous for its barbeque. It was eventually completely "rocked," then finally razed in 1965.

(P218) LENZ HOMOTEL. William & Ethel Lenz opened their 14-room home into a boardinghouse for Route 66 travelers in 1932, remaining open until 1975. Every effort was made (including supplied washcloths, upstairs hallway murals, and home-cooked meals) to make the overnight guest "feel at home."

(P219) CAMP JOY. Started in 1927 as a tent camp (50 cents a night), Camp Joy was one of the first "motels" along Route 66. It was built, owned, and operated by the Spears family for 44 years (1971). The two drive-thru "Camp Joy" signs had messages on the back: "Teach Your Baby to Say Camp Joy," and "Tell Your Friends About Camp Joy." The gas station/grocery store can be seen to the right.

(P220) CAMP JOY. This Sinclair station/grocery store was relocated in town. The community bathhouse behind was moved into the back row of cabins (the roof line is still visible). That's little Joy Spears (named after the camp) in front of her parents (Emis & Lois) and grandparents (Charles & Lida). By 1935 there were 22 cottages, and 24 in 1938 (1, 2, or 3-room) renting from $1.25 - $4 a night. The 1946 AAA Directory of Accommodations listed Camp Joy as "Best here."

(P221) ANDY'S STREET CAR GRILL. Boasting "The Finest Foods In The Ozarks Served Here," the diner, known for "Andy's Famous Fried Domestic Rabbit," was a favorite local eating establishment.

154

(P222) ANDY'S STREET CAR GRILL (Interior). Manager Andy Liebl proudly displays the air conditioned interior of his converted street car. In 1946 the cafe advertised "Lebanon's Best Place For Fine Food." It closed in 1961.

(P223) CARTER & LAWSON BARNSDALL STATION. Built by partners O.E. Carter and Ed Lawson in 1935, the station advertised "We service your car by the latest methods, with celebrated Barnsdall Products." In the early 1940s, Mr. Carter's daughter was able to sit on Trigger, Roy Rogers' horse, who was being transported to California. (Building expansion was done in the 1960s.)

(P224) UNION BUS DEPOT (c.1941). This bus depot, restaurant/gift shop, and Standard station was self-proclaimed to be "The Ozarks Finest." Owner Joe Knight offered a "Hasty - Tasty Sandwich or Steak" to riders on Greyhound, Missouri Pacific, Crown Coach, and M.K.&O. lines.

(P225) UNION BUS DEPOT (c.1941). This "state of the art facility" was opened "24 hours a day, every day." Pictured is the staff on opening day, who once during the war served "a ton of hamburgers in a 24-hour period."

156

(P226) MONTGOMERY MOTOR SALES. Started in 1946 by Hershel Montgomery and his sons Elbert (Ebb) and H.P. (Jude), this dealership sold over 24,000 new and used Cadillacs, Pontiacs, Buicks, Oldsmobiles, and GMC Trucks in the 23 years at this location. Montgomery was also known as "the reliable Route 66 wrecker service" to all those that had problems traveling the historic road.

(P227) NELSON TAVERN. The Texaco station (1926) and hotel (1931) were built by Arthur T. "Colonel" Nelson. On opening day July 3, 1926, the station sent up a "gas balloon at 3 p.m. with a ticket on it good for five Gallons of Gasoline." Nelson's Top O' The Ozarks Camp and landscaped gardens were to the side and rear. The 24 rooms with private bathrooms and kitchen facilities rented for $2 - $3 a night in 1939. All was razed in 1958.

(P228) NELSON'S DREAM VILLAGE. The layout of this "village" came to Colonel Nelson in a dream. After making a sketch the next morning, it was constructed (1934) across the street from his Nelson Hotel and station. The twelve units of native Ozark stone (with bath and kitchen) rented for $3 - $4 a night. A "musical" fountain and light show were in the center courtyard. The "village" remained in business until 1977.

(P229) VIEW OF 66 - LEBANON. This view is looking east toward the Jct. of US 66 & MO 5 (Jefferson), showing the Nelson Tavern (Hotel) and station on the right, and the Union Bus Depot in the background. The "arrow sign" proclaims "Lebanon - 5000 Friendly People."

(P230) CARTER & LAWSON MOBILGAS STATION. Carter & Lawson's second Lebanon station was this Mobilgas store at Jct. Route 66 & Jackson. This photo shows O.E. Carter (L) and Ed Lawson preparing for their 1946 opening with a General Tire sale. Their slogan, carried from their first station in Springfield, was "We Never Close."

(P231) BUNGALOW INN (1934). Owned and operated by Gail & Izola Henson from 1937 to 1946, the Bungalow consisted of the station, restaurant and six cabins. Izola served complete dinners with fresh cornbread for only 35 cents, and made money! The cabins rented for $1 to $1.50 (1938) with community toilets and private cooking facilities (no dishes). All but one cabin (relocated) were razed in the 1950s with highway expansion.

(P232) CAFFEY STATION (1924). This was the first gas station between St. Louis and Springfield on what was to become Route 66 (MO 14). Floyd Caffey later opened a cafe, cottages and a feed mill.

(P233) MERAMEC BARN SIGNS. Pictured are examples of barn advertising that Meramec Caverns used nationwide. The Caverns paid a yearly stipend for the space and maintained the barn roof. These two signs have been used continuously since the mid-1940s on the Millard farm (that served as a construction camp for Old 66 in the 1920s). Nice car!

CARTER & LAWSON'S - UNDERPASS CAFE AND SERVICE STATION
U. S. HWY. 66, PHILLIPSBURG, MO.

(P234) UNDERPASS CAFE/STATION. After a 1941 inheritance by Mrs. O.E. Carter, land was purchased near the Phillipsburg underpass and a metal, pre-fab filling station was built by O.E. Carter and Ed Lawson. The cafe was built in 1950 and Carter & Lawson moved all operations from Lebanon to this site. (The station is no longer standing.)

(P235) UNDERPASS CAFE (Interior). Mrs. Carter left teaching for several years to manage the Underpass. Shown are Mrs. Carter (L) and employees Jessie Larimore, Helen Massey, and Dessie Gilpin. The cafe, known for its home-cooked meals, was a popular stop for many truckers, and a local high school meeting place.

161

(P236) MIDWAY MOTEL. Once called Midway Camp, in 1935 the five units had private cooking facilities, cold running water in the cottage, and community toilets, all for only $1 - $1.50 a night! The motel and station/cafe were added around 1950.

(P237) HARRIS STANDARD STATION. Built in 1930 by S.W. (Sim) Harris. Sim also owned, simultaneously, the Conoco station and cabins on the corner where Central Bank Conway is presently, a Tydol (later Shell) station on the corner now occupied by an insurance agent, and the house (now painted blue) on the fourth corner!

(P238) HARRIS CAFE. Sim's son Barney built the Harris Cafe next to his dad's Standard station in 1931. Barney's wife Marie would cook an entire dinner for 25 cents! Marie also made the Harris Cafe famous as "The Home of the Little Round Pie" - 10 cents!

(P239) HARRIS CAFE. Eventually the cafe (center, minus the door) was enlarged to the right, and expanded to the left to include the rebuilt Standard station. In 1953 the entire complex was moved two miles (toward Phillipsburg) to New 66, later burning down.

(P240) ABBYLEE COURT (c.1940). Originally eight double cabins and a cafe (offering "Meals & Sandwiches"), the Abbylee Court ("Among The Trees") was one of the more scenic motor courts along Missouri 66. This postcard (mailed in 1949) shows the cabin and the "Good Food" cafe that were destroyed by fire in 1950. The court is now monthly rental property.

(P241) SKYLINE CAFE. Built by Herman and Cleta Pearce in 1947 (who had also built the adjoining airstrip) on a site that once had the Main Course Filling Station & Cafe (1929-1931) next to the golf course. Also called Trask's at one time, the Skyline Cafe is on the highest point on Route 66 for a 900-mile stretch. It is rumored that exact spot is somewhere between the cash register and the front door!

(P242) SINCLAIR TOURIST CAMP. A station has operated since the 1920s at this junction of Route 66 (curving left in foreground) and the entrance to the Marshfield business district. Owned and operated by Pat & Robert Abbott from 1946 to 1949 (when photo was taken), the station/cafe/bus stop (and three cabins - $1 a night) was famous for Pearl Bell's pies.

(P243) DAVISON CAMP. Built in the early 1920s by I.C. (Clint) Davison, this was one of the first gas stations between Lebanon and Springfield. The cafe (R) had six stools at the counter and the cabins' kitchens were equipped with electric hot plates. Davison Camp had seven cottages in 1935 ($1 - $1.50) with "electric light all night," and was "Approved by State Board of Health." Shown in Spring, 1929.

(P244) WILLIAMS SERVICE STATION. Winton & Dorothy Williams bought the station from Charley Cafer in 1943. They expanded the station (still standing) and living quarters frequently, staying open seven days a week. When folks from around the country would ask where the Ozark "hillbillies" were, Wint & Dorothy would reply, "You're lookin' at 'um!" That's Wint filling up C.R. MacDonnell's '46 Plymouth.

(P245) 66 MOTOR COURT. Located on what now is a "farm," the Phillips 66 station (razed when the road was widened) was operated by F.C. Tucker and Son. The court went out of business after it was completely bypassed by 4-lane New 66 in 1955. This view is in 1953.

(P246) RED TOP COURT. The Red Top Garage (now used as a church) is the only building that is left of the camp (c.1928) which consisted of a store/cafe with gas pumps, grew to eleven cabins (to the right of the garage) with private toilets, showers, and cooking facilities, and a rather "notorious" roadhouse (to the left), later turned into a skating rink. All the roofs were red, with the garage's roof having "Red Top" painted in white on it.

(P247) OTTO'S STEAK HOUSE. Across from the Red Top, this cafe and Phillips 66 station offered "Breakfast, Home Cooking, Broiled Steaks." It faced original 2-lane 66 (shown here as the "eastbound" lanes after construction of the new "westbound" lanes in 1952). The "new" eastbound lanes were built in 1954, becoming I-44 in 1970. (The house at lower right is still there.)

RANCH HOTEL, 16 MILES EAST OF SPRINGFIELD, MO., ON U. S. HIGHWAY 6(

(P248) RANCH HOTEL. This ranch house was constructed almost entirely from materials found on the Holman Ranch. It became a hotel noted for good food before the establishment of Route 66, and was "the first within several hundred miles of Springfield, Mo., to be listed in Duncan Hines' 'Adventures in Good Eating.' " Holman Ranch also had five cottages. (One cobblestone-foundation cabin remains (c.1920), now used as storage for Exotic Animal Paradise.)

(P249) MCDOWELL MOTORCAR CO. Built by Walter McDowell (1923), the garage faced Pine (old MO 14). It was then expanded to the rear to face new Route 66 after its completion (this view). Through the years it has served as a garage and various car dealerships. The canopy was dismantled in 1937 to provide more room for the larger cars at the Pierce Pennant Oil pumps. That's McDowell's tow truck busy in front.

(P250) ALEXANDER'S DRUG STORE. This drug store, with an ice cream soda fountain, pharmacy, and a doctor's office in back, was also a Greyhound Bus stop. Shown in this 1947 photo are Joel E. Alexander and his daughter Sharon, who later operated her own "penny candy" counter. The pin ball machine was Exhibits "Fast Ball."

(P251) AERIAL VIEW OF 66 - SPRINGFIELD. This 1930s view is to the west along Division (Old 66) showing then-Springfield Municipal Airport (now Downtown Airport), with Glenstone Av (US 66) running left to right at top. The original rock hanger and terminal (1928) still stand. (The trees west of Glenstone were part of Springfield Municipal Golf Course and Drive-A-Mile Driving Range - later O'Reilly Hospital, now Evangel College.)

(P252) CAMPBELL'S 66 EXPRESS. Springfield was the home of Campbell's 66 Express, the Route 66 trucking company owned by Frank Campbell with the logo of the camel "Snortin' Nortin' " painted on the side of their trucks, and who was "Humpin' to Please." (This version still survives on the side of the old headquarters building.)

4¹/₂ Miles East of Springfield, Mo., on U. S. 66

(P253) DOC'S PLACE. This truck stop/cafe backed upon the Frisco tracks and faced Route 66. Doc's was popular locally for their Sunday dinners.

170

Otto's Motel Courts

3 Miles East of Springfield, Mo., on U. S. Highway 66
Steam heated, Otto's Motel Court - Fine Foods

(P254) OTTO'S MOTOR COURTS. Built by Wallace Otto in 1948, Otto's had six "all modern, fire proof steam heated cottages with locked garages. Popular priced cafe." Their motto? "At-Last-A-Place."

Bell's Motel Courts

3 Miles East of Springfield, Mo., on U. S. Highway 66
Steam heated, Bell's Motel Court - Fine Foods

(P255) BELL'S MOTEL COURTS. Otto's became Bell's in January, 1952, when Jerome & Leila Carroll purchased the property. They expanded to 16 units, and became a popular truck stop. (Only six rental apartments remain.) The Bell Motel is still owned and operated by the Carroll family.

(P256) VICTORY COURT (1945). This court, with eight cottages and baths ($3 - $5), offered the traveling public "ultra modern accommodations. New Deluxe cottages, fireproof, perfectly ventilated; insured - cool in summer, warm in winter; knotty pine finish, innerspring mattresses; baths, floor lamps." Victory boasted of "Pure water from our own private well, 635 feet deep."

(P257) TED'S MOTOR COURT. After the name change, the court was owned by Catherine Lipscomb. A new office was added in front, and showers and radios were included in each unit. Still had that 635 foot private well!

(P258) RED ROOSTER MOTEL. The Victory/Ted's motor court finally became the Red Rooster Motel. It now advertised "Free TV, air conditioned." The office was razed for a swimming pool (now drained and grown over). "Rooms from $6." No mention of the well!

(P259) ROCK VIEW COURT. Built by Art Lurvey, brother of Bert (Lurvey's Court), in the 1940s. "17 Units - Tile Bath, Tub & Shower - Beautyrest Foam Pillows - Modern Furniture - Radios - T.V. - Steam Heat - Refrigerated. Quiet units in rear - Playground. 24 hour joining Cafe."

De Luxe Courts — Springfield, Missouri

Located on U. S. 66, 1/2 Mile East of Springfield, Mo.

(P260) DE LUXE COURTS. Accompanied by a Texaco station, this court, built in the 1930s, consisted of "All strictly modern cottages with free lock garages. In 1938 De Luxe had 32 cottages, each with private tub or shower bath - 36 sleeping rooms in all. Furnace heat and refrigerated air-cooled. With or without cooking facilities. Phone, Mail & Telegraph services. Radio in each cottage."

EAGLE TOURIST COURT
SPRINGFIELD, MO.
One-Half Mile East on U. S. 66

(P261) EAGLE TOURIST COURT. One of the first Route 66 tourist courts in the Springfield area, the Eagle had gas pumps, cafe, these three cottages ($1 - $1.50 nightly in 1938) with private kitchen facilities, and the community toilet shown. "Sleep in Safety and Comfort Without Extravagance. All Modern Heated Cottages. Prompt and Courteous Service for Our Guests. Popular Priced Cafe - Famous for Food."

174

REST HAVEN
MOTOR COURT

SPRINGFIELD, MO.

(P262) **REST HAVEN MOTOR COURT.** Built by Hillary & Mary Brightwell in 1947 who operated it until retirement in 1979, and lived on site. Pictured are the first eight units built just after completion. Ten more cottages were added in 1952, and ten more in 1955 when all were "enclosed."

(P263) **REST HAVEN MOTOR COURT.** Within a few years the Rest Haven was "One of the finest of its size in the Middle West. Made of stone construction. Simmons metal furniture with Beautyrest mattresses. Steam heat. Air-cooled. Beautiful tile showers. Service Station and Gift Shop. Restaurant next door.

(P264) REST HAVEN COURT. The "state of the art" sign (with over 900 bulbs!) was added in 1953, and the station was dismantled in 1955 with the relocation of Route 66 to the north. The Rest Haven now offered "100% Refrigerated Air-Conditioning - Telephones - Free Radios - Ice - Newspapers - Well Equipped Playground. Recommended by Duncan Hines."

(P265) CORTEZ MOTOR COURT. Owned and operated by Rex Wilson from 1941-1946, when a AAA directory listed the 16 rooms with baths ($2 -$3.50 a night) as "neat." The court and cafe remained until I-44 bypassed US 66 to the north.

(P266) SPRINGFIELD MOTOR COURT (1947). Built by the Frederick family, later owned and operated by Charles (Bob) & Lois Kubias 1949-1956. "Modern, Insulated, Tan Brick Cottages" with "large rooms and spacious grounds." The motel also advertised something called "Gyramatic Mattresses."

(P267) VIEW OF 66 - SPRINGFIELD. Looking west along Kearney (US 66) toward Jct. Glenstone in Jan., 1956. On the (L), the Springfield Motel (Motor Court), (R) the Cortez Motel. In the distance is the "island" where the first "Historic Route Missouri US 66" sign is located.

(P268) VIEW OF 66 - SPRINGFIELD (1956). This view is east along Kearney (US 66) from Glenstone showing the Springfield Motel, Carl's Cafe, and the Rest Haven Court.

(P269) TRAIL'S END MOTEL (1938). Now the Rancho Court, in the 1950s the rooms of this classic example of a Route 66 court were "Individual Units, Air Conditioned, Steam Heat, Carpeted, Combination Tub and Shower, TV, Room Phones." (A city street now bisects the property.) Great sign!

N. E. CORNER CITY — Jct. U. S. HIGHWAYS 66 & 166 at 65

(P270) ROCK VILLAGE COURT (1947). "One of the finest and most beautiful courts in America. Cottages and 22 unit hotel with newest type fire protection; built of quarried stone and glass brick. Tiled combination tub and shower baths. Recommended by Duncan Hines."

IN SPRINGFIELD, MISSOURI ON U. S. HIWAYS 65, CITY ROUTE 66 AND 166

(P271) MAPLE MOTOR COURT. Owned and operated for years by Howard Williams as "Maple Motel," it offered "Choicest Accommodations. Electrically Heated. Air Cooled or Air Conditioned. Ceramic Tile Baths. Tree Shaded Lawn."

SOUTH WINDS MOTEL

**ON HIGHWAY 65 - 166 - CITY 66 AND JUST SOUTH OF
INTERSTATE 44 JUNCTION 2216 N. GLENSTONE**
"Where Nice People Stay For Rest"

DIAL UN 5-6636

**MR. & MRS. HENRY BUGG - OWNERS
SPRINGFIELD, MISSOURI**

(P272) SOUTH WINDS MOTEL. "Native Stone Cabins. Automatic Gas Heat. 35 Units - Newly Decorated. Family Accommodations. Garages. Playground Equipment."

NEW HAVEN COURTS
ON U. S. 65 AND 66
SPRINGFIELD, MO.

(P273) NEW HAVEN COURTS (1939). Presently called Ozark Motel, the original court of 12 cabins ($3 up) boasted "all strictly modern, fireproof, steam heated cottages. Sleep Safely." A 1946 AAA guide called them "Very good." The Texaco station is gone, but the present motel still consists of the original white-washed rock cottages (with new siding on the front).

180

Skyline Motel
2120 N. Glenstone - Highways 65-166 & City Route 66
Springfield, Mo.

(P274) SKYLINE MOTEL (1950). Now a "motel," the Skyline Tourist Court "In The Heart of the Ozarks," had "T.V. - Telephones - Refrigerated Steam Heat." The stone cottages have been connected and provided with siding.

(P275) GLENSTONE COTTAGE COURT. Originally called Greystone, in the 1950s 4 of the 14 units had kitchenettes. "Automatic heat. TV and air conditioning optional."

(P276) BIG BOY'S AUTO COURT. Built in the 1920s by Al Murphy ("Big Boy" was his nickname), the court had "A beautiful location in the Heart of the Ozarks. Twelve units, strictly modern, some with frigidaires and cooking facilities. Modern Bar-B-Q Restaurant - Super Service Station - Ice Cream Gardens and Fountain. Two minutes to theatre and Shopping District. One Price To All." The sign in front appealed "Hi There. Stop. We've Been Looking For You Today."

(P277) SIXTY-SIX MOTOR COURT. The Dickeys ran this court (built of native stone) whose signs said "Sleep In Comfort," and "Family Accommodations." Sixty-Six Motor Court also had a cafe on site.

Heart of The Ozarks Motel
1801 N. Glenstone
SPRINGFIELD, MISSOURI

(P278) HEART OF THE OZARKS MOTEL. Once called Sixty-Six Motor Court, after the E.R Grainge's became owner/operators the newly-named motel advertised "Automatic Gas Heat - Air Conditioned - Tile Shower - Crib - TV & Radios - Open 24 Hours."

(P279) MILNER HOTEL. Originally the Green Tavern Hotel (1929) that included both a grill (L) and a tavern (R), it became the Milner in the 1940s, then the Missouri Hotel in 1950. The hotel is now used for "transitional housing," the tavern is gone, and the grill is "The Kitchen," a non-profit "food service."

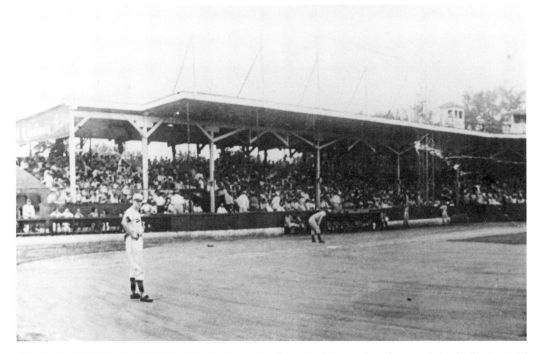

(P280) WHITE CITY FIELD. The St. Louis Cardinals' Triple A minor league club (the Springfield Cardinals) called this home from 1930 to 1942. Stan Musial was just one of the stars. (Babe Ruth played an exhibition game here!)

Greene County Court House, Springfield, Mo.

(P281) GREENE COUNTY COURT HOUSE. Built in 1910 and occupied in 1912, this was the fifth courthouse in Springfield. Fronting on Central Street, the building also housed City Hall on the third floor until 1938, when it moved to the old Post Office building.

(P282) HAMBY'S STEAK HOUSE. Carl Hamby built his Radio Hut Cafe No. 2 in 1946. (The first had been next to a country music station.) Renamed Hamby's the following year, it is still one of Springfield's most popular eating places. Carl continues to believe "...if you don't have a good cup of coffee, you don't have a good restaurant."

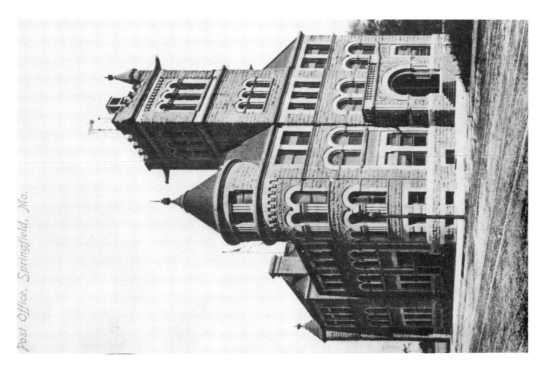

Post Office, Springfield, Mo.

(P283) POST OFFICE (1894). This building housed the federal district court, weather bureau, district marshall, federal district attorney, and post office. It is now Springfield City Hall (since 1938) and also houses The History Museum for Springfield/Greene County. Listed on the National Register of Historic Places.

(P284) AERIAL VIEW OF 66 - SPRINGFIELD. This is a 1948 view of O'Reilly Hospital (now Evangel College) looking east along Division St (Old 66) past Rogers Airport (owned by Francis & Lora Rogers from 1946 to 1954 - now Downtown Airport), and Glenstone Av (left to right - Old 66). Also seen are the Platter Restaurant at the junction, and the old Grove Supper Club (burned in 1979) across from O'Reilly, next to a site that would later be Lily Tulip Cup Corp.

(P285) LILY TULIP CUP CORP. This was one of the first major national companies to locate in Springfield (1952). Its "giant cup" became quite a local Route 66 landmark!

BALDRIDGE MOTOR COURT – Springfield, Mo.

On U. S. 65 - 66 - 166 and City 66, 815 N. Glenstone on east side of City.

(P286) BALDRIDGE MOTOR COURT. Presently the Silver Saddle Motel, this filling station and tourist camp has been owned by John & Hazel Baldridge since 1939. It offered "Tub, Bath or Shower Bath - With or Without Cooking Privileges. We Service Your Car While You Sleep." The stone cottages have been connected with new fronts. Sometimes having to stay up into the morning hours, John proudly says he was never "shut out" (not having at least one patron each day!).

Manhattan DINNER HOUSE 214 S. GLENSTONE SPRINGFIELD, MO.

(P287) MANHATTAN DINNER HOUSE (1947). This "dinner" house served breakfast from 6-10:30 am and dinner from 5-9 pm. Specializing in steaks, the Manhattan remained open into the late 1950s.

(P288) AERIAL VIEW 66 - SPRINGFIELD. This view is looking south at the Jct. Glenstone & St. Louis Street (on the right). Shown is the Rail Haven Motor Court, operated in 1938 by Rex & Mary Wilson. In front of the court is the Wilson Station & Restaurant, built by Rex in 1935, serving groceries and dinners (two tables, six stools). Across Glenstone to the left was the Manhattan Dinner House.

(P289) RAIL HAVEN MOTOR COURT (1938). This was the Rail Haven's first postcard, "Look for the rail fence." A motor court "for motorists who demand the best. Popular haven for women and children." At one time "16 stone cottages with showers, automatic safety controlled gas heat, laundry facilities, children's playground," and "very good beds." By 1946, it had grown to 28 rooms and was considered "excellent" by AAA.

188

(P290) **CORRAL DRIVE-IN RESTAURANT** (1945). "The best of foods served in our comfortable dining room, at our fountain, or in your car. Air Conditioned Dining Room. The Place With the Friendly Western Atmosphere." In 1955 the Corral became a Fisher's Hi-Boy Drive-In, lasting until 1970.

(P291) **ELMHURST MOTEL.** Built in the late 1940s, the Elmhurst remained open until 1965. "Ultra-modern cottages with innerspring mattresses. Nearest Downtown Motel. Only minutes from center of shopping and theatre district. Recreational facilities for the entire family. Good restaurants nearby."

SPRINGFIELD VETERINARY HOSPITAL
1213 ST. LOUIS ST. PHONE 345   SPRINGFIELD, MISSOURI

(P292) SPRINGFIELD VETERINARY HOSPITAL. Built in 1929 by a Dr. Carter, this has been continually operated as a veterinary hospital since. This postcard from the 1940s (advertising "For large and Small animals") shows the business with residence of the doctor upstairs. Present owner Dr. Tedd Hamaker is using this view as a restoration guide.

(P293) COLONIAL BAKING COMPANY (1929). This baker of Colonial Bread (and once "Rainbo" Cake) posed their trucks (proclaiming "Visitors Always Welcome") across St. Louis Street (US 66). In the 1940s and 50s, the bakery erected advertising signs in rural front yards along Route 66 in this area, with a picture of a loaf of Colonial and "is good bread" spelled out, and with the property owner's name below. Several "aged" signs remain.

190

The Kentwood Arms Hotel
Springfield, Missouri

(P294) KENTWOOD ARMS HOTEL (1926). A 5-story hotel built by John T. Woodruff, first president of the National Highway 66 Association. Containing over 100 guest rooms and suites, a barbershop, grill room, beauty parlor, ballroom, and rooftop terrace garden, the Kentwood was a "haven of comfort, luxury, and efficiency for the traveling public." (In 1935, rooms were $2.50 up.) The property is currently owned by Southwest Missouri State University.

(P295) KENTWOOD ARMS HOTEL (1926). A 6-story hotel "created to serve the discriminating traveler."

(P296) SHRINE MOSQUE (1923). The Abou Ben Adhem Shrine Mosque, "one of the outstanding Shrine Mosques in the country. Its auditorium, equipped with large stage and organ, has a seating capacity of 3,600." Its basement bowling alley (existing into the 1970s) was equipped with manual pin setters and opened to the public.

St. Louis Street, Looking West — Springfield, Missouri

(P297) VIEW OF 66 - SPRINGFIELD. This view is to the west along St. Louis Street (US 66) from Kimbrough. The Greyhound Bus Depot (L) (originally the Pierce Bus Terminal) has been regrettably recently razed. The largest building on the left is the Colonial Hotel, in the background is seen the Heer's building on the Square, and the tallest structure (R) is the Woodruff Building. Between the Woodruff and Heer's buildings is the Gilloiz Theatre.

192

Pierce Petroleum Bus and Tourist Terminal
U. S. Highway 66, Springfield, Mo.

(P298) PIERCE BUS TERMINAL. The Pierce Petroleum Bus and Tourist Terminal featured a Pierce Pennant service station and restaurant. St. Louis Street (US 66) was later widened and the terminal became the Greyhound Bus Depot, now razed.

(P299) USO CLUB. The building and park (that faced St. Louis St. - US 66) served as a USO club from 1942-1945. Later the building (facing Benton Ave) became the Townhouse Cocktail Lounge.

(P300) VIEW OF 66 - SPRINGFIELD. Looking west along St. Louis (c.1915), Route 66 went straight, between the Colonial Hotel (L) and Woodruff Building (R), through the Public Square becoming College Street.

(P301) JEWELL THEATRE (1910). Built by Harry Jewell, this theatre housed the Ozark Jubilee, a coast-to-coast country music television show aired live every Saturday night from 1955 to 1960. The Jubilee was hosted by Red Foley, and helped make stars of Brenda Lee, Johnny Cash, Chet Atkins, Mel Tillis, Slim Wilson, Jimmy Dean and Ferlin Husky.

(P302) COLONIAL HOTEL (1906). Now vacant, this grand old hotel had been host to many state and national functions. In 1935 the 150 rooms rented for $2 up. (The hotel is presently owned by Southwest Missouri State University.) The building behind (with archway) was the Baldwin Theater, built in 1891 and destroyed by fire in 1909.

(P303) WOODRUFF BUILDING (1911). This office building was created by John T. Woodruff (first president of the National Highway 66 Association), who also built the Kentwood Arms Hotel (also in Springfield on Route 66). The road on the left is St. Louis (later City 66), leading to the Square.

(P304) GILLOIZ THEATRE. Presently under renovation, this opulent 1,100-seat moviehouse was built by M.E. Gilloiz (at a cost of $300,000) on the route of the newly proposed national highway. Opening night (October 11, 1926) festivities included the feature, newsreel and cartoon (Felix the Cat), live performances by the Swiss Song Bird (from Grauman's Million Dollar Theatre in Los Angeles), and by the Gilloiz Orchestra and "singing organist at the theatre's Wurlitzer pipe organ." On the National Register of Histroic Places, the Gilloiz closed in 1980.

(P305) GILLOIZ THEATRE (Interior). Constructed of a combination of Italian, Spanish, Mediterranean, and art deco motif styles, the theatre played host to at least three world premieres: *The Shepherd of the Hills*, Harold Bell Wright's popular story set in the Ozarks near Branson, *Jesse James*, with Tyrone Power and Henry Fonda, and *The Winning Team*, starring Ronald Reagan (as Grover Cleveland Alexander, the great baseball pitcher who had played with the St. Louis Cardinals), who had brought the debut to Springfield as a tribute to President Harry Truman, who was going to be in town for a reunion.

The Public Square, Springfield, Missouri

(P306) VIEW OF 66 - SPRINGFIELD. This view is from St. Louis Street looking west through the Square toward College Street. Most buildings are pre-1920s. Pictured on the right is Heer's Department Store ("Since 1869"), in this building since 1915. Also on the Square is a historical marker indicating where James "Wild Bill" Hickok shot and killed Dave Tutt in a duel over a gambling debt (1865).

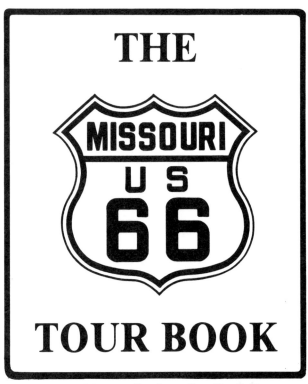

THE

MISSOURI

U S

66

TOUR BOOK

For Additional Copies - See Back Page

(P307) OLD CALABOOSE. Built in 1892 for under $3,000, the Calaboose is now listed on the National Register of Historic Places. (This view is from 1911.) A new jail was built in 1924, but the Old Calaboose was still used as a "holding facility" into the 1960s. It is the oldest remaining public building constructed by the city.

(P308) HAWKINS MILLING CO. Built by Fred Hawkins in 1940, providing "Flour - Feed - Meal," this was also a distributing warehouse for Vitality Dog Food. In 1943, Fred's nephew Max became a partner in the now Hawkins Milling Co. Max's son Jim is the present owner. The road in the foreground is College St (City 66).

Rockwood Court and Cafe

ONE MILE WEST
ON CITY ROUTE U. S. 60 & 66
2204 COLLEGE ST. - TEL. 6-9768
SPRINGFIELD, MISSOURI

(P309) ROCKWOOD COURT (1931). The court advertised "All Units New. One of the finest and most beautiful courts in the city on Highway 66. Strictly Modern. Tubs and Showers. Tile Bathrooms. Restaurant featuring finest foods." Stayed the Rockwood until 1969.

(P310) ROCK FOUNTAIN TOURIST COURT (1947). "One of Springfield's best. Large, spacious grounds, quiet and pleasant, clean and comfortable. Cooled by Friendlier." Called the Melinda Motel since the early 1960s.

(P311) RED'S GIANT HAMBURG (1947-1984). When Sheldon (Red) Chaney was painting his sign, he ran out of room and the "ER" didn't fit. This was the world's first restaurant with a "drive-thru window" with speakers for ordering. On Red's wife Julia's 70th birthday in 1984, she walked out of the kitchen and retired, never to open again. (The only exception: a special auction for local charities of their various products that received orders, "donations," from all over the world!)

(P312) "66" MOTEL. Built in the 1930s, there were originally three cabins (with garages) behind a station/cafe (later Red's Giant Hamburg). Red and Julia Chaney (after enclosing the garages, doubling capacity - renting for $2.50 a night in 1948) operated the motel from 1947 to 1955. The house on the left is still Red & Julia's residence.

TRAVELERS COURT – Rt. 4 West – US 66 – City Route – Springfield, Mo.

(P313) TRAVELER'S COURT. Built in the early 1940s, Russell Carter owned and operated these 30-plus units (some with "Kitchenettes & Freezing Units") during the 1950s. "All Cabins have Showers and Excellent Beds - Large Cabins, some with Private Garages," some with fireplaces. A double unit (now painted pink!) that was on the right of the horseshoe drive is all that remains.

(P314) HILAND DAIRY. This local dairy (still serving the Ozarks) started north of Springfield in 1938. It relocated to the south side of Kearney (Bypass 66) in 1948 (when this photo was taken), then purchased a dairy farm across the street, its present location. Sure like the sign!

(P315) DOLING PARK (1907). Doling Park was a favorite stopping place for Route 66 motorists, featuring a "carnival" with funhouse, rides, bumper cars, skating rink, a boat chute into a lake that is fed by a spring flowing from Doling Cave, and the "best swimming hole in the Ozarks." The lake and park remain.

(P316) BYPASS TERMINAL CAFE. This Barnsdall truck stop/service station and cafe faced the intersection of Bypass 66 and City 66 (Chestnut). Built in the late 1930s, the cafe (owned for many years by Roy & Marie Farley) had "rooms" upstairs and offered Royal Crown Cola, "Best By Taste-Test." Torn down in the late 1970s. The Bypass Terminal Barber Shop still stands.

(P317) WISHING WELL MOTEL (1947). "Spacious grounds, Beautifully furnished. Beauty Rest Mattresses, Locked Garages. Steam Heat or Panel Ray. Reasonable Rates." The original office (on the right) still stands; however, the once-popular well is gone.

Lone Star Court, Route No. 4, W. 66 - Springfield, Mo.

(P318) LONE STAR TOURIST COURT. The converted home/Standard service/cafe, with cabins nestled in the surrounding trees, was locally famous for its "penny candy."

ANDY'S MODERN ROCK COTTAGES, 5 MILES WEST OF SPRINGFIELD, MO., ON U. S. 66

(P319) ANDY'S MODERN ROCK COTTAGES. "Twelve modern rock cottages with accommodations for 44 people. Clean, Insulated, Comfortable, Innerspring Mattresses. Heated." The cafe/station (now Homer's) and several cottages in the back remain.

(P320) THIS OLD HOUSE. George & Elizabeth Wiley (with youngest son William in 1890s photo) built the house c.1850. (The second story was added c.1900.) The house has been in the Wiley family for over 140 years! Delores (wife of Dan, a great-grandson) converted the house into this crafts store that recently was a stop on the Missouri US 66 Association Car Tour.

(P321) VIEW OF 66 - WILEY YARD. This 1927 photo shows James Wiley, son Frank, and grandsons James and Dan working on a concrete mixer with a Route 66 construction crew. The equipment was in the Wiley front yard.

(P322) BARNES & SON GENERAL MERCHANDISE. John Barnes and his son Clell built the 2-story, 34'x36' store in 1934 (selling groceries and such), along with an attached residence below and behind. This 1935 photo shows travelers waiting to be sold some of the "goods" available.

(P323) BARNES GENERAL STORE. The business expanded to provide Sinclair gas and garage services, a barbershop, feed store, mill, slaughterhouse and locker, furniture and appliances. (The station and hardware moved across US 66 in the 1960s.) The Perryman family bought the enterprise in 1972.

SHORTY WEST - GRAYSTONE HEIGHTS
RT. 7, BOX 520, HWY 66
10 MILES WEST SPRINGFIELD MO.

(P324) GRAYSTONE HEIGHTS. Built by Ben Brewer of native stone in 1935, there were six cabins with hot and cold running water, private toilets and showers ($1.25 - $1.75). By 1939 the Graystone had grown to eight "Modern Cabins and Cafe, Air Cooled. Conoco Service." ($1.50 - $3.00). It remained in business until I-44 bypassed Old 66 (mid-1960s).

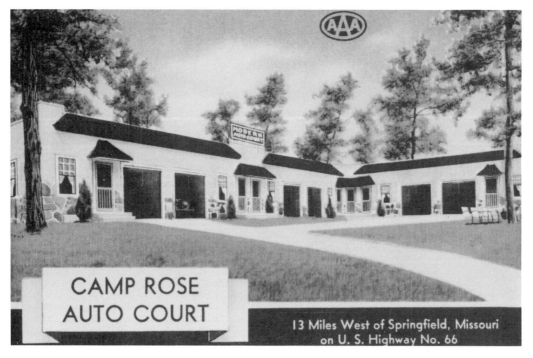

CAMP ROSE
AUTO COURT

13 Miles West of Springfield, Missouri
on U. S. Highway No. 66

(P325) CAMP ROSE AUTO COURT. "All modern, heated, fireproof cottages. Away from all noise and railroad. Good water, playgrounds for children, popular priced coffee shop. One of the coolest spots in the Ozarks." In 1937 the seven cottages rented for $1 - $1.25. The grocery/station building remains.

(P326) HAMILTON, BROWN SHOE CO. Built by A.A. Combs in 1903 of sandstone from the nearby town of Paris Springs. The shoe company ("Keep The Quality Up") also sold Chattanooga plows. Pictured are the operators, D. (Red) & Minnie Combs Fearn. In later years, the building housed a general store, movie theater, and even a funeral parlor!

Why'd They Name It That?

(See page 261)

(P327) VIEW OF 66 - HALLTOWN. This view from 1910 is looking east along what would become US 66. The old Hamilton, Brown Shoe Company building is on the left. In the right background is the Christian Church, still standing (without steeple).

(P328) CAMP LOOKOUT. Promoted as the "Most Modern on US 66," the nine cottages (with private baths) rented for $1.50 - $3.50 (1938). The Phillips 66 service station/garage and cafe foundations remain. "Your Home Away From Home" was "Spotlessly Clean."

(P329) SHADY SIDE CAMP (c.1930). Like many other "camps," Shady Side had a service station/office that later was expanded to include a cafe and grocery. In 1935 the guests in the five cottages (nestled in a grove of oak trees) had "private cooking facilities (dishes not provided) and access to community toilets and showers" for $1 - $1.50 a night. (The small stone structure to the right of the converted station was a pumphouse.)

Log City Motel on U. S. 66 — 14 Miles East of Carthage, Missouri
16 Units—Dining Room—Liquor—"You Name It—We've Got It"

(P330) LOG CITY CAMP (1926). Carl Stansbury built his "dream" business of logs from the property: a gas station/store, several cabins, and cafe. In 1935 the camp advertised "14 modern cottages with conveniences" ($1 - $3). "Dining room and coffee shop air-conditioned by washed air, serving excellent food at popular prices. You Name It - We've Got It." The motel grew to 16 units; only three are left standing.

FOREST PARK CAMP ON HIGHWAY US-66

(P331) FOREST PARK CAMP (1928). A rival of Log City Camp, in 1935 Forest Park had ten rock cabins, a cafe, tavern and dancehall. "Modern Cabins, Gas Heat. A Good Place To Eat. Whitson & Hammond, Proprietors." Always trying to undersell Log City across the road, a rivalry lasted for years.

212

EAST JUNCTION U. S. HIGHWAYS 66 AND 66 ALTERNATE, CARTHAGE, MO.

(P332) WHITE COURT (c.1927). The first building was a cafe/gas station on the far left. Later a total of eight stone cottages were added. They advertised "Cafe in Connection" and "We Service Your Car." The Scotts ran the court from 1957-1987, enclosing the cottages/garages together. The sign (since repainted) dates to the 1940s.

Phone FI 8-2161
Carthage, Missouri

Lake Shore Motel

Frank Tucker
Owner

(P333) LAKE SHORE MOTEL. In addition to good fishing in Lake Kellogg, the Lake Shore offered "Tile Baths - Broadloom - Best of furnished Rooms - Individual Temperature Control (Winter and Summer) - Nice Lobby - Beautiful Location."

(P334) KEL-LAKE MOTEL. Across from Lake Kellogg, the motel advertised itself as "New, Refrigerated Air-Conditioning, Steam Heat, Tile Bath. Free Radios. Commercial & Family Rates."

(P335) JASPER COUNTY COURTHOUSE (1889). Built of Carthage stone, this magnificent courthouse is on the Public Square, just two blocks off Route 66. (Both the square and courthouse are on the National Register of Historic Places.)

214

(P336) BOOTS COURT (1939). Built by Arthur Boots at the "Crossroads of America," the Boots (with a "Radio In Every Room") claimed to be "A new, modern court of 14 units, each with tile shower, floor furnace - heat thermostat control, air conditioned, and garage." It is said that Clark Gable once stayed in room 6! The Boots was a single owner/operator (the Asplins) from 1948-1991.

(P337) BOOTS DRIVE-IN (1946). Arthur Boots also built this drive-in across from his old court. Offering fountain service and "Breakfast at any hour!" In the 1950s, basketburgers, Susie-Q fries, chicken-in-a-basket, and barbeque filled out the menu. The Boots also sold "Souvenirs-Novelties & Gifts." It closed in 1970.

Lakeside Park, Webb City, Mo.

(P338) LAKESIDE PARK. This amusement park was a popular location for summertime activities on the west bank of Center Creek. Nearby was the Lakeside Tourist Camp of six cottages (1935).

(P339) GENERAL MINING SCENE. Typical view of old mining landscape in the Webb City area. It was here on a rainy August night in 1944 that Gilbert Smith's double-deck truckload of hogs (40) tipped over, freeing its cargo to scatter in the fields. Advised not to pursue the pigs in the dark, the men experienced eerie feelings throughout the night listening to the squealing of the hogs as they fell into mine shafts and pits (some 100-300-feet deep!). By morning, only 14 were rounded up!

216

CIVIC DRIVE-IN CAFE   Webb City, Mo.
On 66 Highway From Coast to Coast   71 from Canada to the Gulf

(P340) CIVIC DRIVE-IN CAFE. The Civic Drive-In (with complete fountain service) was the "Tri-States' only Dry Night Club and Restaurant. Dine and Dance on our Side Walk Cafe." The bottom view of this postcard (mailed in 1942) is looking east down Broadway, past the still-present Webb City Bank. (As you left, the overhead sign read, "Thank You - Call Again.")

410 SO. MADISON AVE., WEBB CITY, MO.

(P341) OZARK MOTEL. This "Brand New" motel had rooms with "Rubberfoam mattresses - All tile baths - Individual furnace heat." Along with "Reasonable Rates," the Ozark also had a coffee shop. (Note the US 66 sign to the left.)

Joplin's Newest and Finest Tourist Court"

(P342) FENIX ULTRA MODERN COURT. Situated at "The Crossroads of America," the Fenix advertised "Innerspring mattresses - Tile baths - Kiddies Playground. 15 acres of shady lawn in the heart of the Ozark Playgrounds."

LINCREST COURT AND CAFE, WEBB CITY, MO.

(P343) LINCREST COURT AND CAFE. "Clean, Cool and Comfortable. Eat, Sleep and Gas Up. Mr. and Mrs. T.I. Halley, Prop." (This posrcard was mailed in 1951.)

Main Street, Joplin, Missouri

(P344) VIEW OF 66 - MAIN STREET. This view looking south along Main shows the Hotel Connor (R) (on the present site of the Joplin Public Library), Keystone Hotel (L) (4th & Main), since razed, and the Fox Theatre (L), now Central Christian Center.

(P345) BOB MILLER'S RESTAURANT. This restaurant (shown in a postcard mailed in 1950) was the "District's Newest - Most Modern - Air Conditioned." It specialized in "Steaks, Fried Chicken, Salads and the Best in Pastries. Food You Will Remember."

On Highways 66 & 71, East City Limits, Joplin, Mo.

(P346) TWIN OAKS COURT. The Twin Oaks Court was "The Place to Sleep." The Twin Oaks Cafe had "Just Good Food."

ELMS MOTEL

(P347) THE ELMS MOTEL. "Joplin's finest. 25 beautifully furnished, fireproof cottages, on spacious grounds. Wall to wall carpeting. Tile showers. Free Radios. Vented Wall Heaters. Some Units Air-Conditioned. Free Ice, & Kiddies Playground." Whew!

(P348) THE COLONEL'S RESTAURANT. The original sign (now "The Colonel's Pancake House") is atop a fireplace-expanded business that assured you of "quick, efficient service on your choice of all varieties of pancakes, hickory-smoked Bar-B-Que, chicken, steaks and seafoods."

(P349) EAST 7TH STREET MOTEL. "Seventeen Units (17). Family Rates. Air-Conditioned, Automatic Heat, Thermostatic Controlled, Shower and Tub Bath, Radio & Television." Proclaimed "Good eats close by."

"We Stopped Here Last Night"

(P350) CASTLE KOURT. Built in the early 1940s, the "Kourt" expanded to 24 cabins, then 35 "cottages," each with "Bath and Beauty Rest Mattresses, Private Garages." Finally, Castle had 40 units, all "Air-Conditioned - Phone and Radio in Each Room. Courtesy - Cleanliness - Comfort."

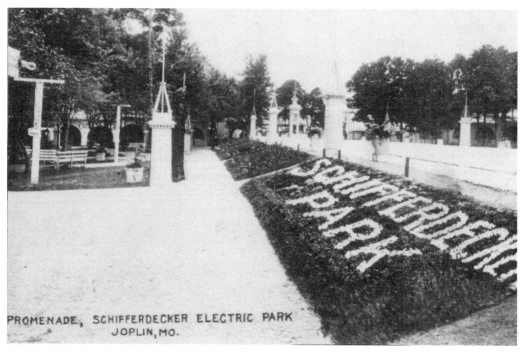

PROMENADE, SCHIFFERDECKER ELECTRIC PARK
JOPLIN, MO.

(P351) SCHIFFERDECKER PARK. Charles Schifferdecker, a German immigrant who amassed a fortune in Joplin mining, ice, and beer & bottling, donated this land to the city in 1913. The park is 160 acres of rolling prairie and woodland, containing an 18-hole golf course (green fees in 1941 were 35 cents!), Mineral Museum, the Joplin Historical Society, and a replica of an 19th century tavern (from Pea Ridge, AK). Pictured is the old Promenade of the "Electric Park" in the 1930s.

THE

MISSOURI US 66

TOUR BOOK

Joplin to St. Louis

JOPLIN. (Pop. 40,866). **Named to honor the Rev. Harris G. Joplin, who established the first Methodist congregation in Jasper County in 1840. By an act of the state legislature in 1873 (brought about by some local "skirmishes"), the communities of East Joplin, West Joplin, Murphysburg, and Union City were merged under the name Joplin.**
A few miles to the southwest, at the juncture of Missouri, Kansas and Oklahoma, is the "Tri-State Spook Light," a still unexplained phenomenon dating back before the turn of the century.

Enter Missouri on "Old Route 66." State Line Bar & Grill (L) (c.1925), originally a restaurant/honky-tonk. Liquor store (L) that was Gray and Archer Filling Station (c.1925). Remains of Gillead's Barbeque (R) (c.1945) and Shady Rest Motel (R). Jct. 7th Street (MO 66). Left, 2 miles past Schifferdecker Park (L) **(P351)** and 66 Pit Stop Lounge (L), once Dixie Lee's Dine & Dance Bar (c.1930). Pride Motors office (L)(2403 7th) that was part of Castle Kourt **(P350)**. West 7th St Apts (L)(2207), once Little King's Hotel Court, built in the 1930s and advertising "Good eats close by." Wal-Mart (L)(1717), site of the Koronado Hotel Kourts, "Our Rooms and Coffee Shops are Air Conditioned by Refrigeration." Station and tire store (L)(200 block) that was originally the Ozark Filling Station (1925).

Jct. Main & 7th Streets.
(Main Street was, during the old mining days, a rather bawdy place, as witnessed by an ad for the old House of Lords, saying it offers "... fine cuisine, gambling, and 'soiled doves.' " The site is now a park.) Joplin was a large lead and zinc mining area in the

19th century, and there have been numerous cave-ins of the city streets (caused by a labyrinth of abandoned mine tunnels under the city), creating various US 66 routes through town.

1) CITY 66.

Left on Main. View of 66 (**P344**). Office (R)(419), once Bob Miller's Restaurant (**P345**). Right on 2nd Street (Broadway) to 1500 block. Left on St. Louis, over the new Turkey Creek bridge, right onto Euclid 1/2 mile to Utica. Barber shop (R) that was the Shamrock Inn, Gas Station/Cafe (c.1930). Right on Utica to stop sign (N Florida Ave). Across Florida (R), the old 2-story Royal Heights Apartments (c.1930), then Joplin Little Theater for awhile. Left to Zora. Right to Range Line (stop light). Across the road (L), Coach's Corner, on the site of Lincrest Court (**P343**). Cross Range Line one block. Left on Jefferson (City 66).

[*NOTE: Jefferson (City 66) is soon interrupted by MacArthur Blvd (MO 171).*]

Turn left to Jct. Madison Ave & MacArthur (MO 171). McDonald's (410 Madison), on the site of the old Ozark Motel (**P341**). Cross MacArthur, turn right then left back onto Jefferson. Continue 1/2 mile to Jct. Broadway & Jefferson, in Webb City. (See next page.)

2) ALTERNATE 66.

Left on Main. View of 66 (**P344**). Office (R)(419), once Bob Miller's Restaurant (**P345**). 5 miles to MacArthur Blvd (MO 171). Right, 1-1/2 miles. Angle left onto Powell Street to Broadway. Right on Broadway to Jct. Broadway & Jefferson, in Webb City. (See next page.)

3) BYPASS 66.

Straight on 7th Street 2 miles, past Bob Owen Auto Center (L)(1902) that occupies the site of East 7th Street Motel (**P349**), to Range Line (US 71). On the (L), site of the old Elms Motel (628 S Range Line) (**P347**).

[Right here 1/2 block to The Colonel's Restaurant (R) (**P348**).]

Left on Range Line to Jct. 4th Street. Ben Franklin Crafts parking lot (R), site of Twin Oaks Court (401S) (**P346**). Jct. Zora Ave (2600N), Coach's Corner (R), site of Lincrest Court (2601N) (**P343**). Just past Oaklawns business office (L)(2700N) was the site of Fenix Ultra Modern Court (2710N) (**P342**). Jct. Madison Ave & MacArthur Blvd (MO 171). McDonald's (L)(410 Madison), on the site of the old Ozark Motel (**P341**). Cross MacArthur to Broadway, right 1 block to Jct. Broadway & Jefferson, in Webb City.

WEBB CITY. (Pop. 7,449). **After "discovering" lead in his cornfield in 1873, John C. Webb created a mine, made money, and plated the town later named for him.**

Jct. Broadway & Jefferson.
East on Broadway to Webb (stop sign). Jog left on Webb 1/2 block to Jct. Webb & Broadway. On the (L), Professional Plaza building, once Civic Drive-In Cafe **(P340)**. Right on Broadway, past the Webb City Bank through town. Remains (L) of the wood frame Daugherty Street Filling Station (c.1930). Right at stop sign through the abandoned mines and piles of slag (chat - waste from lead and zinc mines) **(P339)**.

CARTERVILLE. (Pop. 2,013). **Named for J.L. Carter, one of the men who laid out the town in 1875. During W.W. I, Carterville was a prosperous city of 12,000, but then the mines shut down.**
Continue through town to Pine Street (400 block). Left 1 mile to the yield sign (Carterville Cemetery). Right 1 mile past Lakeside Park **(P338)** to the "double-arch" bridge over Center Creek (1926). Straight 1-1/2 miles to 3-way Jct.

[*NOTE: Old 66 (which is cut off 1/2 mile further by US 71), went straight, passing behind the 66 Drive-In to Municipal Park.*]

Right, over US 71, then left on outer road (Oak Street) past the front of 66 Drive-In Theatre (L) (1945) to Municipal Park (R) (1937).

CARTHAGE. (Pop. 10,747). **Established in 1842, the town was named for ancient Carthage, a model of democracy. Carthage was the capitol of the marble industry at the turn of the century. The Missouri State Capitol, U.S. Capitol, and even the White House are all faced with the stone. Carthage was also the home of Belle Starr, the notorious "Bandit Queen."**
Continue on Oak to Jct. Garrison Ave. In town, the Square and the Jasper County Courthouse **(P335)**, both on the National Register of Historic Places. Left on Garrison, past the Boots Court (L) **(P336)** and, across the street, the old Boots Drive-In **(P337)**, now an insurance business.
Jct. Garrison & Central Avenues. Right on Central (City 66) 1-1/2 miles, veering left onto MO 96 and the Frisco Railroad balustrade bridge (1934), over the Spring River bridges (1923) to Jct. MO 96 & CO. V. Kel-Lake Motel (L) **(P334)**. Lake Shore Motel (R) **(P333)**.

Jct. MO 96 & CO. V
Odometer Notation: (0.0m)

[*NOTE: New 66 (MO 96) goes straight here 2 miles to Jct. Old 66*]

Right on Old 66 by Kellogg Lake Park, then left, past Red Rock Apartments (L), originally White's Court **(P332)**, and, 1/2 mile on the (R) across from a trailer court, a stone building (that sold barbeque) associated with the old Sunset Drive-In (early 1950s-late 1960s). The ticket booth and concession stand (now a converted barn) still stand.

(1.5m) Jct. MO 96 (New 66). Right.

[*NOTE: In the 1950s, towns along US 66 from here to Halltown threatened to sue the government i* *they lost the "US 66" designation to "I-44," the newly proposed 4-lane interstate highway to be buil* *over Route 66. The highway department made the decision to change the proposed route of I-44 to* *the south, following US 166 (completed 1962-1965), thus bypassing this stretch of road* *Subsequently, Old 66 was rebuilt (1956) to meet new standards, razing many businesses, and, ir* *1972, lost its "US 66" status anyway, being redesignated MO 96.*]

(9m) AVILLA. (Pop. 146). **Laid out by D.S. Holman and A.L. Love in 1858, and named for Avilla, Indiana, their hometown.**

(12m) STONE CITY (R) and **(12.5m) LOG CITY (R).** **These towns were known for their popular resorts frequented by many from Carthage and the surrounding area, and named for their materials of construction.**
Across from Log City **(P330)** are the old cabins of the rival Forest Park Camp **(P331).**

(14m) PLEW. **For years known as Plewtite, the town was named for a local family in 1893.**

(16.5m) Remains of Shady Side Camp (L) **(P329).**

(17m) RESCUE. **In the late 1800s, a family traveling out West had their wagon break down. Locals took them in for the few days it took for repairs. Afterward, the family said they were lucky to have been "rescued." The area's well-deserved reputation accounted for the new post office's name in 1897.**
Cabins, lodge, and station (L), built by a Mr. & Mrs. Roy Rogers in the 1920s (not that one!); later Reed's Cabins.

(21m) PHELPS. **Named for Colonel Bill Phelps, a famous local attorney for the MoPac Railroad, and the lobbyist who obtained a post office for the town in 1857.**
Henson Building (L) (c.1924) (now a residence), once had a cafe, store & barber shop, with rental rooms upstairs. What's left of Bill's Station (L) (c.1926). **(22.5m)** Group of gray buildings (R) that was the Welcome Inn (c.1940), once a tavern (then restaurant) with cabins in back.

(25m) Jct. MO 39. ALBATROSS. **A village established in 1926 and named for the transcontinental Albatross Bus Lines that stopped here. Like other towns on Route 66, Albatross grew with the highway into the 1950s (six gas stations).**
Miller's Station (R), once Morgan's DX (c.1945). The old Albatross Store (R) (c.1930) with an addition (1949) that is now an auto body shop. Remains of Carver's Cabins (L), with an old station in front.

(27m) HEATONVILLE. In 1868 Daniel Heaton laid out a town on his property and named it for Daniel Heaton. The post office was called Heaton from 1872 to 1881. Treasure Corner (R), once D.L. Morris Garage (1936), built on the site of the Heaton post office. **(27.5m)** Remodeled buildings (R), once Castle Rock Courts (1931), consisting of a filling station/restaurant and tourist camp. **(29m)** Jct. CO. M (to the south). **(29.5m)** Left onto Old 66 - Farm Road 2062 (runs parallel to MO 96 for 2 miles). **(31.5m)** Cross over MO 96. House (R) among the foundation ruins of what was Camp Lookout **(P328)**. Continue on a stretch of original Route 66 surface.

(32.5m) SPENCER. Spencer's Store was on the site of the old Johnson's Mill, and in 1868 the post office was named for the store. The existing buildings (L) date to the early 1920s. Steel thru-truss bridge (1926) over Johnson Creek. Left at first road (CO. N), 1/2 mile to Jct. MO 96 (stop sign). Cross MO 96. Turnback Creek bridge (1923).

(34m) PARIS SPRINGS. Named for E.G. Paris, local hotel proprietor, in 1872. The "healing" waters of the nearby springs brought about the formation of the Paris Springs Bottling Co. The town moved south 1/2 mile to its present location, and is now called Paris Springs Junction. Stone garage (R) (c.1944). The old Gay Parita Store (R) (c.1930) with cafe, grocery and service station. Cobblestone garage and station (L) (c.1926). Continue straight on MO 266 2 miles to the remains of White City Motel (L) (c.1950), once consisting of 10 cabins with garages encircling an office/residence. Bridge over Billies Creek (1923).

(37m) HALLTOWN. (Pop. 161). **George Hall settled in the area in 1870, opened a store, and in 1879 named the new post office after the storekeeper. Halltown is now known for its many antique shops.** Aerial view of 66 **(P327)**. Richard's Antiques (L) (c.1906), once a livery and meat packing business, next door to the old Hamilton, Brown Shoe Co. **(P326)**. Remodeled building (L) that was Stone's Corner Station (1927), once owned and operated by Ted & Marjorie Stone. Halltown Flea Market (L) (West's Grocery) (1922). The old Las Vegas Hotel and barber shop (R) (c.1930), built by Charlie Dammer with silver dollars he had won in Las Vegas. Whitehall Mercantile, Jerry & Thelma White's antique store (L), built (1900) as a grocery with fraternal and community functions upstairs. Continue east on MO 266.

(41m) Jct. Farm Road 45. **PLANO. Probably named for Plano, Texas (now part of Dallas), with which there had been a great deal of trade. A post office from 1895 to 1903.** Remains (L) of a casket factory/mortuary; later a furniture store. Rock residence (R), once a grocery store/Tydol gas station. **(42.5m)** Building (R) on far side of new bridge over Pickerel Creek that was a part of Camp Rose **(P325)**, on a stretch of Old 66 (now bypassed). **(45m)** R&J Floral buildings (L) that were Graystone Heights **(P324)**. Continue 1/2 mile to Jct. CO. T.

[Four miles to the left is **BOIS D'ARC. The name is French for "wood of the bow" (now commonly called "Osage Orange"), the strong, pliable hedgeapple tree local Indians used for weapons. From 1847 to 1868, the town name was spelled as it was pronounced: "Bow Dark."**]

Stone buildings (L) that were the O'Dell gas station and cafe. **(46.5m)** Barnes General Store (R) **(P322, P323)**. Remains (R) of Moore's Sinclair/Texaco filling station and two cabins (idle since the early 1970s). This Old House (L) **(P320, P321)**. Homer's Body Shop (L) that was part of Andy's Modern Rock Cottages **(P319)**. Cross I-44.

SPRINGFIELD. (Pop. 140,494). **The "Queen City of the Ozarks," and the "Birthplace of Route 66," Springfield was originally a settlement called Campbell and Fulbright Springs. It is generally accepted that during an election to name the new town in 1833, James Wilson (for whom Wilson's Creek, the site of a great Civil War battle, was named) offered a "pull" from his freshly-made white whisky to any who would vote for his choice: Springfield (after the beautiful little town in Massachusetts where he was born).**
Springfield was the home of Campbell's 66 Express **(P252)**. Seven Gables Restaurant (L)(4500 block), once a 2-story building in the 1920s. It exploded and burned in the early 1950s and was rebuilt, still with a 7-gabled roof. Best Budget Inn (L)(4433 Chestnut), once the Lone Star Tourist Court **(P318)**. Jct. Chestnut Expwy & US 160 (West Bypass). On the (R), the Wishing Well Motel **(P317)**. On the (L), a Git 'n' Go station on the site of the Bypass Terminal Cafe **(P316)**.

Jct. Chestnut Expwy & US 160 (West Bypass). There are two basic US 66 routes through Springfield (and an alternate route through "North Springfield"): 1) CITY 66 (below); 2) BYPASS 66 (page 230).

1) CITY 66. *(Recommended Route)*
Straight on Business Loop 44 (Chestnut Expwy). Trantham's Bait Shop (R), next to what's left of Traveler's Court (3134 Chestnut) **(P313)**. Remains of Red's Giant Hamburg (R)(2846) **(P311)** and the "66" Motel **(P312)**. Right on College Street Melinda Court (R)(2400), once called Rock Fountain Court **(P310)**. Shamrock Square Motel (R)(2300) (1935), now Stanford Square. Ginny Lee's Restaurant, Motel & Pub (R)(2204), originally Rockwood Court **(309)**.
Jct. Kansas Expwy. The old Rainbow Garden Court (R) (1930). Across the way (R) is Hawkins Milling Co. **(P308)**. Continue 2 miles to Square.

[*NOTE: City 66 (College Street) went straight through the Square, becoming St. Louis Street, but is now cut off.*]

Veer right onto McDaniel Street, past the Old Calaboose (L) **(P307)**, to Park Central South (South St), left into the Public Square (most buildings pre-1920s). (L) Marker indicating where Wild Bill Hickok shot and killed Dave Tutt in a duel over a gambling debt (1865).

NOTE: *To take* **Alternate 66** *(1931), round Square past Abundant Life Center, once the Fox movie theatre, and exit on the north (Booneville St.). City Hall (R)* **(P283)**. *Greene County Courthouse (R)* **P281)**, *and across the street (L), Hamby's Steak House* **(P282)**. *World Headquarters of the Assemblies of God (L) (in Springfield since 1918), built on the site of White City Park Stadium* **P280)**. *Jct. Commercial Street. Right, through "North Springfield" and its historic, albeit deteriorating, architecture. This entire district is listed on the National Register of Historic Places. The town, incorporated in 1871, had as its first "mayor" James J. Barnard, consolidated with Springfield in 1887. Jefferson Avenue Footbridge spanning the Frisco tracks (L) (1902). Missouri Hotel (R), previously the Milner Hotel* **(P279)**. *The Frisco Railroad Museum (L) in the old Dispatcher's Building (1943), the only such facility devoted exclusively to the St. Louis-San Francisco Railway. Continue 1-1/2 miles to* Jct Glenstone & Commercial (see below).]

Exit Square to the east (Park Central East - St. Louis St.). Gilloiz Theatre (L) **(P304, P305)**. Woodruff Building (L) **(P303)**. Colonial Hotel (R) **(P302)**.

NOTE: *City 66 (St. Louis Street)* **(P300)** *is now cut off by "Ozark Jubilee Park on Historic Old 66," site of the old Jewell Theatre* **(P301)**.]

Right, then left on McDaniel, veering back onto St. Louis Street. Mercantile Bank (L), site of the old USO grounds **(P299)**. Lot (R), site of Pierce Bus Terminal **(P298)**. View of 66 **(P297)**. Abou Ben Adhem Shrine Mosque (L) **(P296)**. The old Kentwood Arms Hotel (R)(700 St. Louis) **(P294, P295)**. Colonial Baking Company (R)(1028) **(P293)**. Oriental restaurant (L)(1135) that once was Gus Otto's Eat Shop, reviewed by a 1946 AAA guide as "much better than its exterior indicates." Jct. National Ave. Springfield Veterinary Hospital (L) **(P292)**. Dillon's market (R)(1260), the site of the Elmhurst Motel **(P291)**. Empty lot (L)(1300 block), site of the old Corral Drive-In Restaurant **P290)**. Continue across the railroad tracks five blocks to Jct. Glenstone. Aerial view of 66 **(P288)**. Rail Haven Motel (Cottage) (R) **(P289)**. Across Glenstone (R) by a station was the Manhattan Dinner House **(P287)**. Left on Glenstone Ave. Cross Chestnut Expwy (Business Loop 44). Silver Saddle Motel (L), originally Baldridge Motor Court **P286)**. The old Lily Tulip plant (R) **(P285)**. Evangel College (L), on the site of the W.W. II O'Reilly Army Hospital **(P284)**.

Jct. Division St (CO. YY).

NOTE: *Division Street (CO. YY) was the original Route 66 to the east until Kearney St (MO 744) was constructed further to the north. To follow, turn right, past the Springfield Downtown Airport (R)(2200 block)* **(P251)**, *over US 65, to Jct. MO 125. Left, to Jct. CO. OO (Old 66). Right, into Strafford.*]

Continue north on Glenstone to next stop light.

Jct. Glenstone & Commercial.

Pizza Hut (L), on the site of the Sixty-Six Motor Court (**P277**), later Heart of the Ozarks Motel (**P278**). Brown Derby/Bass Pro Shop (R), where Big Boy's Auto Court (**P276**) once was. North on Glenstone. Glenstone Cottage Court (L)(2023) (**P275**). Skyline Motel (R)(2120) (**P274**). Ozark Motel (L)(2137), previously New Haven Courts (**P273**). McDonald's (R)(2220), site of the South Winds Motel (**P272**). Maple Motel (L)(2233) (**P271**). Best Inns (L), once Rock Village Court (**P270**). Jct. Glenstone & Kearney (MO 744) (see below).

2) **BYPASS 66.**
Left on West Bypass (US 160) 2 miles, under the railroad overpasses (1935), past the Rex Smith Gas Station (originally a "Flying A" station/cafe with cabins in back) that has been operated by the same family since 1932, to Jct. MO 744 (Kearney St). Right 3-1/2 miles, past the Traveler's Motel (L) (early 1940s), to Doling Park (**P315**) turnoff (L)(9300) (Robberson St). Continue east 1-1/2 miles, past Hiland Dairy (L)(1133) (**P314**) and Rancho Court (R), once Trail's End Motel (**P269**), to Jct. Glenstone & Kearney (MO 744).

Jct. Glenstone & Kearney (MO 744).
Odometer Notation: (0.0m)

[Prior to proceeding east, turn left one block to see an example of a classic Route 66 motel: Rancho Court (L), once Trail's End Motel (**P269**).]

East on Kearney (US 66 - MO 744).

[Missouri was the first state to enact a bill (1990) declaring Route 66 a historic highway. This is the site (R) of the first sign erected identifying the road.]

Views of 66 (**P267, P268**). K Mart (R), site of the Springfield Motor Court (**P266**). Wal-Mart (L), site of the old Cortez Courts (**P265**). Rest Haven Motel (R) (**263, P264, P265**). Jct. Barnes Ave. Empty field (R), site of the Eagle Tourist Court (**P261**). Across the road, the Furniture Factory Outlet (L)(2209), site of the Deluxe Courts (**P260**). East end of Lurvey's Plaza parking lot (L)(2300 block) was Rock View Court (**P259**). The reopened Holiday Drive-In (L). Remains of Lurveys Court (L)(2900), built by Bert Lurvey in the 1930s, rocked after W.W. II. Cross over US 65. Bell Motel (R) (1948), originally Otto's (**P254, P255**). Across the road, apartments that were previously Victory Court (**P256**), Ted's Motor Court (**P257**), and Red Rooster Motel (**P258**). The old SoMo Center (R), now Stiles Roofing, on the site of Doc's Place (**P253**).
(6m) Farm Road (FR 209). Dutch's Tavern (L). **NOGO. A junction on the Frisco Railroad into the 1940s, Nogo had a post office from 1896 to 1907. When locals gathered to name the "town" (two stores and a blacksmith shop), there wasn't agreement on any one name. Someone opined that the meeting was a "no-go," a popular phrase of the day. Nogo was then selected.**

(7.5m) STRAFFORD. (Pop. 1,166). With the coming of the railroad in 1870, a town was platted on land that had been a Kickapoo Indian reservation, and named for J. Strafford, a local landowner from Strafford, Connecticut. Strafford was listed in *Ripley's Believe It Or Not* as the only American town with 2 "main streets" and no back alleys. (MO 14, one block to the left, was the main road in town until Route 66 was built between the railroad and the backs of the businesses, which were then extended to meet the new road.)
Continue past Jct. MO 125. Wee World Daycare (L), once Alexander's Drug Store **(P250)**. A-1 Garage (L), once McDowell Garage **(P249)**. Straight on CO. OO.

(12m) HOLMAN. The Holman family owned land here, creating a store and post office in 1903. Behind the low cobblestone wall (R), Holman Woods consisted of cabins and the Ranch Hotel & Restaurant **(P248)**.

(15.5m) Site of the old Red Top Court (R) **(P246)** and Otto's Steak House (L) **(P247)**. Continue down a lovely one-mile winding section of Old 66, past the **NORTHVIEW** turnoff (CO. B).

(20m) MARSHFIELD. (Pop. 4,374). The seat of Webster County, the site was surveyed in 1855 and named for Daniel Webster's Massachusetts home, Marshfield. According to the 1941 edition of the W.P.A.'s *Missouri*, since the tornadoes of 1878-1880 (which killed over 80 townspeople) "things have gone fairly quiet, with only the rise and fall of farm prices to affect the town's tranquility."

(21m) Jct. MO 38. On the (R), across from Singer Auto Parts, was 66 Motor Court **(P245)**. Straight, past Tony's Fastop (L), once William's Service Station **(P244)**, and the Conoco station (L) that was Davison Camp **(P243)** to Jct. CO. CC. Country Express station/store, once Sinclair Tourist Camp **(P242)**. Left onto CO. CC - Hubble Drive (honoring local son Edwin Hubble, the first astronomer to prove the existence of other galaxies, and for whom the Hubble Telescope, launched into orbit in 1990, is named). Main Course Cafe (R), once Skyline Cafe **(P241)** by the golf course. **(25.5m)** Pony truss bridge (1924) over the Niangua River, and an old Phillips 66 station (R) (1925). House with cabins (R), once Oak Vale Park (1939-1952), before that Carpenter's Camp, with cafe/service station and outdoor facilities for cooking and picnics (now being restored by owner Alf Smith). Rock home (R) that once was Rockhaven Roadhouse & Cabins (c.1925), the area's "most popular night spot for beer and dancing" in the 1930s and 40s.

(27.5m) Jct. CO. M. **NIANGUA.** (Pop. 459). The town was named after the river, which was probably so-called for the Indian phrase "ne anoga," which translates "water that runs over a man." Locals say "Niangua" comes from another phrase meaning "I won't go away," or "I won't go farther," suggesting that this was where one would settle.
Niangua Junction Service Station/Grocery (L) (c.1935-remodeled 1992). Abbylee Modern Court (R) **(P240)**. The old Timber Hill Camp (L) (c.1935), once three cottages with private cooking facilities, community toilets and showers, renting for $1 - $1.50 (The residence in front was the office.)

(30.5m) Jct. CO. HH. **SAMPSON** (R). **At one point there was a store/post office (1904 1935) and gas station among a few cabins.**
On the far side of the Frisco tracks is part of an old tomato canning factory, one of 1? along the railroad between Marshfield and Cuba operated by Case Canning Co. o Marshfield. In the early 1930s, there were over 300 canning factories here in Webste County alone!

(35m) CONWAY. (Pop. 629). **Named for a J. Conway, who was responsible for getting th railroad here in 1869.**
Jct. CO. J. Empty lot across the road (L) that was the site of Harris Standard Statio (**P237**) and Harris Cafe (**P238, P239**). Straight on CO. CC.

[*NOTE: Old 66 crossed to left of I-44 at* **(39.5m)** *by Midway Motel (L)* (**P236**) *and Skelly station.*]

(40m) PHILLIPSBURG. (Pop. 170). **Named for Rufus Phillips, who built a store her prior to the Civil War.**
Phillipsburg School and Gymnasium (R) (1937-burned in 1985). Jct. CO. C. Left, ove I-44 to CO. W (Old 66). Right. Building (L) that was the Underpass Cafe & Statio (**P234, P235**). Frisco Railroad underpass (1926), referred to as the "subway" when i was built. Many a car transport truck had to let air out of their tires to pass under Example of barn advertising (L) by Meramec Caverns (**P233**).

[*NOTE: Old 66 crossed to the right of I-44 at* **(44.5m)**.]

(45m) CAFFEYVILLE. Named for J. Floyd Caffey, local businessman (P232). The 4-lan New 66 razed most of the town.
Old 66 ran in front of the stone Liberty Freewill Baptist Church on the right of I-4 (1950s - on this site since 1907).

[*NOTE: Old 66 crosses back I-44 at* **(46m)**.]

Grouping of trailers (R) just before county road X44-716. Site (R) of the ol Bungalow Inn (**P231**). 1/10th mile further is a relocated tan-colored cabin (residence (R), closest to road, that was moved from the Bungalow Inn . **(48.5m)** Slab bridg over Goodwin Branch (1922).

(49m) LEBANON. (Pop. 9,983). **Created in 1849 to be the county seat of Laclede County it was named for Lebanon, Tennessee, from which many of the settlers had come. Harold Be Wright, author of** *The Shepherd of the Hills,* **and pastor of the First Christian Church, began hi literary career in Lebanon.**
B&D Truck Port sign ("Self Service Entrance") from Vesta Court east of town. Jct Business Loop 44. Left 2 miles, past Colt Market (L), once Mobilgas station (**P230**) Jct. MO 5. View of 66 (**P229**). Consumer's Market (R), site of Nelson's Tavern (**P227**)

and Country Kitchen (L), site of Nelson's Dream Village (**P228**). Across the intersection (L) is the Metro office building, once the Union Bus Depot (**P224, P225**).

[Leave US 66 here to the left 1-1/2 blocks to a Kentucky Fried Chicken restaurant with an extensive Route 66 photo display, and, next door, Lebanon Yamaha, once Montgomery Motor Sales (**P226**).]

Continue on Elm, past the Orchard Farms liquor store (L) that was originally a Barnsdall gas station (**P223**), Drake Automotive (L), on the site of Andy's Street Car Diner (**P221, P222**), "apartments" (L), once Camp Joy (**P219, P220**), and the old 3-story Lenz HoMotel (L) (**P218**). (**53m**) Left on Old Highway 66 (Seminole). Wrink's Market (L) (1950), originally built to be a 2-story hotel, but never completed. Remains of Clark's Rock Court (R) (**P216, P217**). Munger Moss Motel (Motor Court) (R) & Restaurant (**P214, P215**). Just after jog in road (due to relocation of 66) is Cromer's Motors (L), on the site of Scotty's Tourist City (**P213**). Hall-Moore Stuff Co. (L) in an old dairy farm barn built of native stone (1928). El Rancho mobile home park (L) that was Vesta Court (**P211, P212**). Village Oaks (L), once 4-Acre Court (**P210**). Remains of Satellite Cafe & Phillips 66 station (L) (**P209**).

[*NOTE: Old 66 is cutoff by I-44 at* (**57.5m**).]

(**58.5m**) Jct. CO. F.

[To the left is the town of **SLEEPER. Named for the Frisco construction gang foreman James Sleeper, who had run a rail spur to a coal shute where the town was later built (1883).**]

Turn right on CO. F, over I-44, curving around to Outer Road. Left 2 miles past the remains of the slab bridge on the old road to Sleeper (L) (county road X44-331). Across from an old "Riley's" sign (L) is a trailer that was next to the site of what was Riley's Snack Bar (**P207, P208**). Jct CO. T & CO. N. Rock building (L) that was part of the Harbor Cafe & Cabins (**P204, P205**), later Geno's (**P206**). Continue east on CO. N.

[*NOTE: Old 66 crossed to the left of I-44 at* (**64.5m**) *(just before CO. N turns right), past a grouping of remodeled buildings that was Sunrise View Tourist Court* (**P203**), *followed the power poles, and cut back to the right at* (**66.5m**), *by the remains of Eden Resort (R)* (**P202**).]

Continue to the Gasconade River. (The French in St. Louis conferred the name Gasconade on an area inhabited by "boastful" settlers who reminded them of a similar group of braggarts from Gascony, back in France.)

[*NOTE: The twin New 66 bridges were built in 1956.*]

Cross steel thru-truss bridge (1922) over the Gasconade River.

[*NOTE: Prior to 1922, the Gasconade was crossed at Beck Ford (under what is now I-44), accounting for the sharp right angle in the "new" present road*]

(68m) HAZELGREEN. A post office from 1858 to 1958, Hazelgreen got its name from the many local hazel nut bushes. The town used to have lodges, stores, many homes, and a school. By 1955, 4-lane New 66 had been built through town.
Cleared site (R) (after last house) of what once was Walker Bros. Resort **(P199, P200)**. Across the road was Parsons Lodge **(P201)**. Hazelgreen Cemetery (R) (1840s). **(69m)** Wayside Inn (R), built to be Hancock's Motel (c.1945).

(69.5m) GASCOZARK. The name is a combination of the Gasconade River and the Ozark Mountains. (Ozark is a simplified spelling of the French "Aux Arc." Aux is pronounced "oh," meaning "to," and "Arc" is short for the Arkansas Indian tribe. Ozark: "to the Arkansas.")
The old Gascozark Cafe (L) **(P197, P198)**. Across the road (R) is the Gascozark Trading Post that was Caldwell's Cafe & Court **(P194, P195, P196)**. Continue east on CO. AB 1-1/2 miles to road AB 347 (L).

(71m) DADTOWN. "Dad" & Betty Lewis built a general store and grist mill here in the early 1900s, and the "town" was named to honor him. His son Marion set up a large tent nearby, featuring the first silent movies the area had seen.
Empty buildings (L) that were Central Motel & Station **(P193)**. Straight 2 miles to the old Spring Valley Court (R) (1929). The small building in front was the "shower room," and the remodeled house was the store & cafe. Travelers would stop and water their stock (later, cars) from the spring below. Route 66 Flea Market (L). **(76m)** Jct. CO. AB & CO. AA.

LAQUEY. "Lake way" was named for Joseph J. Laquey, who had used his influence to get a post office established (1898) in Parsons Store (Laquey Market).

[*NOTE: The original blacktopped route went left on CO. AA 3 miles, right on CO. P through town, joining MO. 17. The "new" paved version of 66 went straight on CO. AB to MO 17 (2 miles) to Jct. CO. P.*]

Continue straight on CO. AB to North MO 17, past Jct. CO. P. **(78.5m)** Vern Smith's old Hillcrest Groceries & Station (R) **(P192)**. Across the road was the site of the Normandy **(P191)**.

(79m) BUCKHORN. Originally called Pleasant Grove, it was renamed for the Buckhorn Tavern where stagecoaches stopped on the road from Springfield to St. Louis. (There was a sign over the door with a large pair of antlers.)
Pleasant Grove Cabins & Cafe (R) **(P190)**. Crafts & gifts store (L) that was D&D Cafe and Market **(P188, P189)**. Directly across the road on the (R) is a church that was Pleasant Grove Christian Church, built in 1926 and serving continuously as a church since. **(79.5m)** Jct. I-44.

NOTE: Old 66 went straight past the S&G Motel, but is now cut off 1 mile ahead.]

Left, over I-44. Right on MO. 17.

NOTE: Old 66 crosses back to the left at **(81m)**.]

82m) WAYNESVILLE. (Pop. 3,207). **In 1834 the new post office was named for Gen. "Mad Anthony" Wayne, hero of the Battle of Stony Point during the American Revolution. He is reported to have told Gen. George Washington, "I'll storm Hell if you'll plan it!" The town was the chief recreational center for Fort Leonard Wood personnel during the war. (84.5m)** Ed Wilson Garage (R), once Bohannon Cafe & Garage (1934). Funeral home (L), once Bell Hotel Resort **(P187)**. Cross the Roubidoux Creek bridge (1923) (pronounced "rue-bee-due," and named for an early French fur trader). Victory Tavern/Waynesville Cafe (R) **(P186)**. On the Square, Pulaski County Courthouse (L) **(P185)** and the Old Stagecoach Stop (L), built in pioneer days, both on the National Register of Historic Places. Continue east on Business Loop 44.

86m) ST. ROBERT. (Pop. 1,730). **Rev. Robert J. Arnold established a Catholic church outside Fort Wood in an area that had previously been known as Gospel Ridge. The church, and later the town that developed (1951), were named for his patron saint: St. Robert Bellarmine.** Follow Business Loop 44 (Old 66) over I-44. Phillips Oakwood Quick Shop (L), once Oakwood Village **(P184)**. The Ranch Motel (R) **(P183)**. George M. Reed Roadside Park (L) (dedicated 1955). Jct. Missouri Ave (CO. Y - entrance to Fort Wood). Ramada Inn parking lot (L), site of the old Scott Garage **(P182)**. Straight on CO. Z, past rental units (L) that were Tower Court (mid-1940s). **(91m)** Jct. CO. Z & MO 28.

NOTE: Old 66 crossed to the left of I-44 here, through what once was **MORGAN HEIGHTS**. *(In 1935 there were six cabins here renting for $1 - $1.50 a night.) At the "Y" of Old 66 and MO 28, there is a secluded "unused" section of the old road* **(P181)**. *Old 66 then crossed back to the right of I-44 by the Devil's Elbow Motel and Grand View Market.*]

Continue east on CO. Z.

NOTE: CO. Z, the 4-lane blacktopped New 66 (completely paved in 1945), was built during W.W. II to facilitate traffic to Fort Wood. This was the first-used and last-replaced (1981) 4-lane section of Route 66 in Missouri.]

92m) Devil's Elbow Motel (L) **(P180)** and Grand View Market (L).

NOTE: Original 2-lane 66 crosses CO. Z from the left. 4-lane New 66 (CO. Z) goes straight, over the Big Piney River to Jct. with 2-lane Old 66, thus bypassing Devils Elbow.]

Veer right on Old 66, past Grandview Court (L), once Clinton Cabins then Easy Inn (1932). Scenic Overlook (R). View of 66 **(P179)**. Wind down the hill past the stone house (R) fronting River Park, once Graham's Resort **(P178)**.

(93.5m) DEVILS ELBOW. The name was given to a severe point on the Big Piney River by lumberjacks trying to float hand-hewn railroad ties downriver to the town of Jerome. They feared and cursed the bend in the river (caused by a large boulder locals say was put there by the devil) that resulted in inevitable log jams, saying it was a "devil of an elbow!"
Site (R) of the old Devil's Elbow Cafe **(P174, P175)**. Allman's Market (R), once Miller's **(P176)**. Next door, the old McCoy's Store & Camp **(P177)**. Continue to the Big Piney River. (The Big and Little Piney Rivers owe their name origins to the pine forests along their banks that provided the first important commercial timber in the state.) Cross the steel thru-truss bridge (1923) over the Big Piney River. Spectacular bluffs! (Listed by the State Planning Commission as one of the seven beauty spots in Missouri). The old Munger-Moss Sandwich Shop (Barbeque) (L) **(P171, P172)**, later Elbow Inn **(P173)**. **(94m)** Jct. CO. Z (stop sign) **(P169)**. Remodeled home (R), once Heatherington's Cabins station/store/bus stop. Behind and above the remodeled store are the remains of the chimney of the "Honeymoon Cottage." Roubidoux Woodworkers (L), once Dale's Sporting Goods **(P170)**.

[*NOTE: Old 66 went straight here, around the hill to the right into Hooker, but is now cut off.*]

Right on CO. Z (New 66), through the famous "Hooker Cut" **(P166, P167, P168)**.

(95m) HOOKER (L). A post office from 1900 to 1955, the town was originally called Pine Bluff. It was later named Hooker (for a local landowning family), as was Hooker Hollow and Hooker Ford. At one time Hooker had a concert band, and, as the *St. Louis Post-Dispatch* reported in 1929, "Missouri's Smallest High School."

[*NOTE: Old 66, now dirt, came from the (L) around the hill, past Fancher Store* **(P165)** *and ran along the left of CO. Z, following power poles, past the Hooker church and cemetery* **(P164)**.]

Across from the entry into Hooker, buildings and residence (R) that were the Hillbilly Store **(P163)**.

(96m) SPRINGVALE (L). Named for its topographical characteristics, this area had some homes/cabins, along with a service station, cafe, and saloon.

Continue east on CO. Z, rejoining Old 66 (2-lane), to Jct. CO. J.

[*NOTE: Old 66 is cut off 1/2 mile further.*]

Left over I-44. Right on North Outer Road East (Powellville Outer Rd).

[*NOTE: Old 66 crossed to the left of I-44 from in front of the stone building (R) that was Bennett's Catfish Cafe* (**P162**).]

(97.5m) CLEMENTINE. Also known as "Basket Ridge," it became a popular tourist stop along Route 66 for the many stands selling homemade Ozark baskets and novelties, many strung on wires paralleling the highway. A post office was started here in 1891.
Remains of Fisher's Filling Station (R) (c.1935), once with several cabins in back prior to Route 66 relocation (1952). Onyx Mountain Caverns (L), used for centuries by Native Americans, and advertising "The Largest Indian Shelter Room in Missouri." **(99m)** Circle dirt drive (L) marking the site of **POWELLVILLE** (**P160, P161**). Cluster of trailers around a concrete slab (L) was the site of Pecan Joe's (**159**). Wind down into the valley. View of 66 (**P158**). **(101m)** First road (R) is Jct. I-44.

[*NOTE: Old 66 went straight here, through Stonydell* (**P157**), *and crossed the Little Piney River at Arlington.*]

ARLINGTON. Laid out by P.C. Harrison and probably named for his hometown in Virginia. Some suggest Arlington was a "corruption" of Arlie, wife of the first storekeeper. The town predates Route 66 and served railroad travelers and vacationers. Due to county lines being redrawn through the years, Arlington has successively been in St. Louis, Gasconade, Crawford, Pulaski, and Phelps counties.

[*NOTE: Old 66 went right, under the New 66 bridges, wound up the hill and around to the left, crossing between the I-44 lanes by what was Beacon Hill Motel* (**P156**).]

Right, cross over I-44, left onto the interstate, continuing over eastbound bridge (1966) (westbound-1952).

[*NOTE: Old 66 crossed to the middle of the I-44 lanes 1/2 mile past bridge.*]

Aerial view of 66 (**P153**).

[*NOTE: Old 66 crossed to the south outer road after top of hill.*]

Home on left, with cabins from the Totem Pole Trading Post (R) (**P154, P155**). On New 66 access road (L) (I-44 north outer road) are the remains of John's Modern Cabins (c.1935), once consisting of six cabins, a filling station, cafe/novelty shop, and washroom. They were moved to the left to accommodate the widening of Route 66. Vernelle's Motel & Restaurant (L) (**P152**). **(105m)** Leave I-44 at Sugar Tree Road Exit 176. Right, then left, rejoining Old 66 (Arlington Outer Rd). **(107.5m)** I-44 Flea Market (L), once T&T Cafe (**P151**). Luther Mathis' Garage (R) (early 1900s). Log home (L), site of Towell's Store (**P150**).

(108m) DOOLITTLE. (Pop. 599). **The area called Centerville (halfway between Newburg and Rolla) was renamed and dedicated in 1946 to honor Gen. Jimmy Doolittle, W.W. II flying hero (and Medal of Honor winner), who flew his own bomber to the ceremonies.**
Grouping of buildings (L) that were the original Bennett's Catfish & Cabins **(P148, P149)**. Malone's Service Station (L) **(147)**.
Jct. CO. T, **NEWBURG** turnoff. Straight 1/2 mile.

[*NOTE: Old 66 crossed to the left of I-44 between Ramsey's Garage and Cabins (R) (c.1941) and Lou Hargis' old skating rink (R), part of his tourist camp (1944), then back to the right* **(110m)** *from behind Gauntlet Paint, once the "new" Totem Pole* **(146)**.]

(110.5m) Aaron's Radiator Service (R) **(P145)**. Home (L) that was Aaron's Old Homestead **(P144)** and log cabin (L). Beaver Creek bridge (1922), now considered to be a one-lane bridge! Rebuilt residence (R) that was Hillside Tavern (late 1920s), once with gas pumps in front and cabins in back. A popular Route 66 tavern/nightclub from the 1930s to 1955, when fire damaged the upper floor.

(112m) MARTIN SPRING. **Prior to Route 66, the nearby springs watered horses and livestock. The area became known as Martin Spring after William Martin opened a store and springhouse (P143).**
Continue east on Martin Spring Drive, past a water slide (R), site of an old tourist court from the 1930s operated by Walt Levine. (The office is still standing.) Newest location of the Totem Pole Trading Post (R) (1978).

(113.5m) ROLLA. (Pop. 14,090). **When this Pacific Railroad construction town was named in 1858, it is widely believed that locals, many from North Carolina, accepted the suggestion of George Coppedge to name it after Raleigh, his hometown. It was spelled as he pronounced it, "Rolla."**
Jct. Business Loop 44.

[*NOTE: In 1954 the 4-lane New 66 was built around town.*]

EITHER: Follow Business Loop 44 to Jct. Bishop Ave (Original 66). Cross Bishop on Kingshighway (City 66), angle into 6th Street, 3 blocks to Pine. Left on Pine. Phelps County Bank building (R), originally the Hotel Edwin Long **(P142)**. Boatmen's Bank building (L) (8th St.), once Rollamo Theatre **(P141)**. Library (R), once the old Post Office **(P140)**. Uptown Theatre (R) (1940). University of Missouri-Rolla campus (L) (1871). The Western Historical Manuscript Collection has an office on campus that maintains Route 66 memorabilia and papers that is open to the public, (located in room G-3 of the Curtis Law Wilson Library). Continue to Jct. Bishop & Pine.

OR: Follow Business Loop 44 to Jct. Bishop Ave (Original 66). Left on Bishop. Hardee's and Dairy Queen restaurants (L)(1300 block), on the site of the old Phelps Modern Cottages **(P139)**. Continue to Jct. Bishop & Pine (next page).

Jct. Bishop & Pine. East on Bishop (Old 66).
View of 66 (**P138**). Budget Apartments and Denny's (L), on the site of Schuman's Tourist City (**P137**). Aerial view of 66 (**P136**). Jct. Cedar Rd. Amoco station (L), site of the old Trav-L-Odge (**P135**). Lee's Fried Chicken (R), the site of the Colonial Village Hotel (**P134**). The Shell station (R) was the site of the Pennant Tavern (**P132**) & Cafe (**P133**). Aerial view of 66 (**P131**).

Jct. Bishop & I-44.
Odometer Notation: (0.0m)

Cross over I-44 on US 63 (Old 66) 1/2 mile, past Drury Inn (R) where the Sinclair Pennant Hotel was (**P130**).

Jct. RD 2000. **NORTHWYE.** (Pop. 135). **Named for the "Y" created by the junction of US 63 and Route 66, north of Rolla.**
Right, past the union hall (R) built on the site of Ramey's Cafe (**P129**) 1/2 mile to the "To I-44" sign (RD 2020).

[*NOTE: Old 66 (RD 2000) went straight here, but is cut off 1 mile further, and is under I-44 for another 3 miles.*]

Veer left on RD 2020, 3-1/2 miles to Jct. CO. V. Mule Trading Post (R) (1958 - started in Pacific, MO in 1948). Follow "Old Hwy 66 Outer Rd" east.

[*NOTE: Old 66 rejoins outer road at* (**4m**).]

Route 66 Motors (L), originally Delano Thrifty Service and Thrifty Inn restaurant (**P128**). Country Aire (L), once Dillon Court (**P127**). Residence (L) that was Rock Haven Restaurant & Cabins (**P125, P126**).

[*NOTE: Old 66 crossed to the right of I-44 at* (**8m**).]

(**8.5m**) **ST. JAMES.** (Pop. 3,325). **The first settlement was called Big Prairie. In 1860 the name was changed to honor Thomas James, who owned the nearby Maramec Iron Works. It was considered more modest to name a town after one's name-saint - in this case, St. James the Apostle.**

(**9.5m**) Right at stop sign (MO 68) and cross I-44, past the Missouri Veterans Home (L) (1896). Jct. CO. KK (Old 66). Johnnie's Bar (R), originally Rose Cafe (**P124**).

[*NOTE: To the right is Old 66 (cut off 1 mile back) along the divided, tree-lined James Blvd (a public improvement project undertaken when US 66 was routed through this part of town.*]

Left on CO. KK. St. James Auto Repair (L)(103) that was the first of the Delano Oil Co. stations (1930). Jackson Automotive Service (R)(320), once a Delano station (**P123**). Jct. Mueller St (400 block). Building (L), next to propane tanks, is all that remains of the Atlasta Service Station (**P122**). Jct. Springfield (R)(600 block). Building (R), set back from road, that was the St. James Inn (**P121**).

(15m) ROSATI. Settled in 1890 and known as Knobview, in 1930 the local Italian wine growers changed the name to honor Bishop Joseph Rosati, the first Italian bishop of St. Louis. For years there have been many grape stands along Old 66 (**P120**). Jct. CO. F & CO. ZZ. Straight on CO. ZZ.

(19m) FANNING. Named for the four Fanning brothers, who had worked across Missouri on the railroad construction crews before settling here in 1887.

(22.5m) CUBA. (Pop. 2,537). In 1857, two gold miners returned home from California via Cuba and expounded on the island's virtues. Impressed, the townspeople called their new post office "Cuba."

[*NOTE: This section of Route 66 was one-way eastbound from 1953-1968 (New 66). The westbound lanes were part of what is now I-44.*]

Route 66 Lounge (L), originally the West End Tavern (1951). (This has been the site of a tavern since the 1920s.) The old B&M Cafe (R)(700 block) (**P119**). At stop light, title company and law firm (R) that was the Peoples Bank (**P118**). Old 66 Cafe (R) (early 1950s). Peoples Bank (R), site of Barnett Motor Co. (**P117**). Jct. Franklin Blvd (MO 19). The old Midway (L) (**P116**). An old Phillips 66 station (R) (1930s), once operated by the father of Don Carter, the famous St. Louis bowler and member of the Bowling Hall of Fame; later (1940s) Carr's Standard Service and Pontiac Dealership. Continue east, past the Cuba Dairy Creme (R)(402) that opened in 1952 as a Dairy Queen, then changed in 1970 by then-owner Fritz Sthrotkamp. Hotel Cuba (R)(500 block) (**P115**). Wagon Wheel Motel (L) (**P114**). Across the road is what used to be the Red Horse Cabins (**P113**). Across from the water tower is the Paul's Cafe building (L) (**P112**). On the (L)(1000 block), Cuba Self-Storage, site of the Lazy Y Camp (**P111**). Continue past Jct. CO. UU 1/4 mile.

(26.5m) HOFFLIN. Hofflin was named for local landowner William Hofflin. A post office from 1903 to 1943; remaining are the foundations of the general store and gas pumps (P110).

(30m) Jct. CO. H. Oak Grove Wayside Park (L).

[Leave 66 here, through **LEASBURG,** to go to Onondaga Cave (**P109**).]

Bridge over Shallow Creek (1924).

(33m) BOURBON. (Pop. 1,188). **In the early 1850s, newly imported bourbon whisky was sold by Richard Turner at his store to railroad construction crews. The business became known as the "Bourbon Store," and eventually the new town was called Bourbon.**
Across from the high school, a residence (R) that was Hi Hill Station **(P108)**. 1/2 mile on the (R), the old Bourbon Lodge **(P107)**. 1/10th mile on (L), drive marked "066-550," the old Marge & Bernie Station **(P105, P106)**. At stop sign, Peoples Bank (R), site of Tiners Place **(P104)**. Follow the "Old Highway 66" signs around town, by the famous "Bourbon" tower across I-44 **(P103)**, and past the old Roedemeier Garage (L) **P102)**. Cross Jct. CO. J & N. The old Friesenham Dairy Farm (L) **(P101)**. (Allison) Hill (originally Bourbon) Cemetery (L) dating from the 1840s.

(39.5m) SULLIVAN. (Pop. 5,661). **In 1859 the town name was changed from Mount Helicon to thank Stephen Sullivan, who had laid out a new town, given land for the Frisco depot, and had even built the station himself.**
Shamrock Court (Motel) (R) **(P100)**. Jct. CO. D.

[*NOTE: Old 66 is briefly cut off here.*]

Continue to first block (R) (Elmont Rd). Right, to Jct. W. Springfield Rd (Old 66). Scott Welding (R) (1940s), once Standard Garage (1927), opened 24 hours a day with four mechanics on duty, and Sull-Mo Music, once Westgate Manor (1926). Left, past the "Sunny" Jim Bottomley Park (R), named for the former St. Louis Cardinal baseball player (and Hall of Famer) who set the major league record for most RBI's in a single game-12 (1924). To the (R) at stop sign is an insurance agency that was Juergens Station **(P99)**, and the Chamber of Commerce building, once Campbell Chevrolet Dealership **(P98)**. St. Anthonys School (L), site of the Sullmo Hotel & Cabins **(P97)**. Drug store (R), on the site of the old White Swan Restaurant **(P96)**. Cross Jct. MO 185 1/2 mile to a yellow/gold house and trailers (R) on the site of Martha Jane Farm Auto Court **(P94, P95)**. Winsel Creek bridge (1922).

(46m) STANTON. **Originally Reedville, the town was renamed for the Stanton Copper Mines, owned by John Stanton (c. 1856).** Hideout Cavern City Court (Motel) (L) **(P93)**. Stanton Motel (L)(across I-44) **(P92)**. Antique Toy Museum (R), in an old Stuckey's Restaurant. Jesse James Museum (R), in business over 30 years. Jct. CO. W.
[Leave 66 here (R), on CO. W, to see Meramec Caverns **(P91)**.]

[*NOTE: Old 66 is cut off 1/2 mile ahead. It continued next to the railroad (at times under the I-44 eastbound lane) for 3 miles.*]

Left, then right on North Outer Road East. Happy Acres Home (L), once Shady Rest Court. Empty building (L) at Lollar Branch Rd was once the Motel Meramec **(P89)**.

[*NOTE: Old 66 crossed to the left of I-44 at **(50m)**, by the Whispering Pines Estates.*]

Remains of Benson's Tourist City (L) **(P88)**.

[*NOTE: Old 66 crossed to the right, past the old Trade Winds Motel, and back to the left by the si of The Tepee (L)* **(P87)** *and Ozark Court (L)* **(P87)**.]

(51.5m) Jct. St. Louis Inn Rd. On the (R) a salvage yard, site of Leroney's **(P85)**.

[*NOTE: Descending "Coal Mine Hill" to I-44 Rest Area (site of old coal mines), Old 66 swung o under the I-44 westbound lane, curved left up and around the hill, and at the top crossed to the rig! following the railroad tracks, past a house that was the 2nd location of Ozark Rock Curios* **(P84** *into St. Clair (at times under the eastbound lane).*]

(54.5m) Jct. CO. WW. Agape House (L), once Scully's Sunset Inn **(P82, (P83)**.

[*NOTE: Old 66 continued east from here between the tracks and eastbound I-44, past the St. Cla Motel* **(P81)** *into town.*]

Jct. MO 30.

(55m) ST. CLAIR. (Pop. 3,917). **Called Traveler's Repose (after a wayside inn & tavern the name was changed so others wouldn't think of it as a "pioneer cemetery." It was rename for a resident civil engineer of the Frisco Railroad in 1859.**
Cross over I-44 to stop sign (Old 66).

[To the right along Old 66 (now cut off by I-44) is Ritter & Sons Garage (R) **(P79 P80)**, once Shady Shell **(P78)**.]

Turn left on MO 30. Business (R) that once was Harty's Dine-O-Tel **(P77)**. Veer left o North MO 47 (Commercial) to the blinking light. Buildings (L), once The Chuck Wagon cafe & St. Clair Chronicle **(P76)**. Apartment building (L) was the old Hi Spo Motel **(P75)**. Coldwell Banker Realty (R), once Johnson's (Art's) Mo-Tel Cabins **(P73 P74)**. Jct. MO 47 & CO. TT. Straight on CO. TT. Napa Auto Parts (R), once Le Claire Motors **(P72)**. Jct. CO. AH.

[*NOTE: Old 66 has been cut off as it angled left up across the valley.*]

Left, over I-44. Right on North Outer Road East.

[*NOTE: Old 66 rejoins outer road at* **(60.5m)**.]

Wind down the road into the valley. Group of buildings (L) that was the Four Seasons (1927), once comprised of a gas station, tavern and cabins built by Tom Hoff. It was the first local business on the newly paved US 66.

(62m) HALL'S PLACE. During Prohibition, Frank Hall, a local bootlegger, built his "community" here, a house, Sinclair gas station and store (L) (1930). He also had a "bar & barn" dancehall, and at one time, he boasted, seventeen stills (P71).
Continue on outer road.

[*NOTE: Old 66 is now under I-44 for 1 mile.*]

(63m) What's left of the 41 Mile Post (R) (1930s), once consisting of a tavern, store, and cabins. Oak Grove Tavern (L) (1928), a store/tavern with Sinclair pumps in front, and four cabins in back, now expanded into homes.

[*NOTE: Old 66 again swung out under I-44, then moved left of the outer road, along the power poles. It then cut down through the valley and over the Bourbeuse River (pronounced "burr-bus," French for "muddy") on what was the westbound portion of the "Twin Bridges"* (**P70**).]

Jct. US 50. Straight onto CO. AT and over the river. U-Store-It units (R), once the Pin Oak Motel (**P69**). Keys Twin Bridge Cafe and station (R) (1945). Buildings (L) that were Hobbleburger's Tavern, Cafe & Grocery (L) (c.1940). Guffey's Store (R), once the office/grocery for Stropman's Camp (c.1928).

(66.5m) VILLA RIDGE. (Pop. 1,865). A Mr. Emerson, supervisor of the railroad construction in the 1880s, named the new station for the ridge that forms a watershed between the Meramec and Missouri Rivers; and "villa," Spanish for town.

(68m) Child care center (R) that was the old American Inn (**P68**). Sunset Motel (L) (**P67**). Tri-County Truck Stop (L), originally Diamonds Restaurant (**P66**). Jct. MO 100. Straight on East MO 100 (Old 66) past the old 2-story Mingle Inn and Wayside Farmers Market (R) (**P65**). Cross over I-44. Brush Creek Cemetery (L) with gravestones dating to the 1830s. Gardenway Motel (R) (**P64**). El Paso Auction/Trading Post (L), once Cozy Dine Cafe (**P63**). On the new Diamonds property (L) is the site of an old Missouri Highway Weight Station (**62**). Across the road, the Missouri Botanical Garden's Shaw Arboretum (R) (1925), 2400 acres of cultivated trees and plants (opened to the public in 1940), designed to preserve for the future a typical example of Ozark landscape. View of 66 (**P29**). Jct. MO 100 & I-44.

(71.5m) GRAY SUMMIT. (Pop. 2,505). At one time called Point Labadie, it was renamed for Daniel Gray, who kept a hotel here (1841), the highest point on the railroad between Jefferson City and St. Louis.

From Gray Summit, there are three basic US 66 routes through St. Louis: 1) ORIGINAL CITY 66 (below); 2) CITY 66 (page 246); 3) BYPASS 66 (page 249). To best experience the feel of Route 66, it is recommended the motorist use a combination: ORIGINAL CITY 66 to Jct. Manchester Road & Kirkwood. Right on Kirkwood (BYPASS 66) to Jct. Watson Road & Kirkwood. Left on Watson (CITY 66) through St. Louis.

ST. LOUIS. (Pop. 396,685). A town was laid out in 1762 by Pierre Laclede and dedicated to St. Louis IX, name-saint of Louis XV, then King of France. St. Louis IX was the devout and gallant French king in the 13th century, referred to by historians as the "Crusader King." The "Gateway to the West," St. Louis has been under three flags in its history: Spanish, French and American. Home of the Gateway Arch, St. Louis is the largest city on Route 66 between Los Angeles and Chicago.

1) ORIGINAL CITY 66. *(Recommended Route)*

[*NOTE: This was the primary route from 1926 to 1932. "Manchester Road" (MO 100) went from Gray Summit to St. Louis, where it became Market Street (used by fur-trading Indians and farmers taking their produce to market).*]

Jct. MO 100 & I-44.
Odometer Notation: (0.0m)

Left over I-44 on MO 100 (Manchester) through Gray Summit 1/2 mile to Jct. CO. MM.

[Leave 66 here 1 mile to the left to Purina Farms, with domestic animals and activities open to the public since 1925.]

Bel-Air Awning (L), once Tucker Hill Transfer (c.1923), owned by Gene and George Smith who lived in houses on both sides of the business. Residence with enclosed porch (R)(Rd 105 242) that was Summit Cottage **(P51)**. Climb Tucker Hill to top of ridge, past Bahr Discount Foods (L), on the site of the old Motor Inn **(P50)** to Jct. MO 100 & CO. OO (R) (Manchester Road to the left) **(6m)**. Left on Manchester (Old 66), over the Fox Creek bridge (1923) to Jct. MO 100.

[*NOTE: Old 66 crossed to the right of MO 100 here, and ran parallel for 2-1/2 miles.*]

Left on MO 100.

(8.5m) HOLLOW. A relay station for the old St. Louis & Jefferson City Stage Line. For a time, the settlement was known as Dutch Hollow, for "Mine Host Dutch Charles," as Charley Pfaffath, who conducted a popular tavern (R) (now West County Horsemen's Club) in this small valley, was familiarly known.

The old Manchester Road Garage (R) (c.1932). Jct. Melrose Road (Woodland Meadows to right). Left on Melrose, then right on Manchester (Old 66).

(11.5m) FOX CREEK. A post office from 1833-1904. Although the settlement was located at the headwaters of Wild Horse Creek, it was named for the nearby Fox Creek (which was so-called by a local hunter after he had shot an extremely large fox there). The new MO 100 cut through what was left of the town. Not much remains.
Ace Case building (R) that was Fox Creek Garage **(P49)**. Cross Jct. MO 100.

(13m) POND. Settled in the 1820s, it was first called Speer's Pond, for Cyrus Speer, a local millowner.
On the (R) is part of the Big Chief Hotel **(P47, P48)**. Pond Hotel (R) (c.1840), now a residence. Pond Inn "Tavern" (R) **(P46)**. Cross Jct. MO 109.

(14.5m) GROVER. Once known as St. Friedling, a post office was awarded the town during the administration of Grover Cleveland, and renamed in honor of him. The Calvery Christian Church (L) is the site of "Hill Side View," a roadhouse and grounds that overlooked a curve in Old 66 where the contestants of the 1928 "International-Trans-Continental Foot Race" **(P45)** spent the night.

[*NOTE: Old 66 curved left here as you start to climb the hill. A 1/4-mile stretch is visible (L) angling up the hill. It then crossed back to go under MO 100.*]

(15.5m) Jct. MO 100 (Manchester Rd - Old 66). Right.

(16.5m) ELLISVILLE. (Pop.6,233). William Hereford established a post office here in 1843, and probably named it for his hometown in Virginia. Some believe the name honored the man who later developed Ellisville, Vespuccio Ellis, longtime United States Consul to Venezuela.
Cross Jct. MO 340 (Clarkson Rd).

(18m) BALLWIN. (Pop. 21,816). Named for John Ball, who had platted a town in 1837 on his farm near Fish Pot Creek.

(20.5m) WINCHESTER. (Pop. 2,077). Incorporated in 1935, the name is a combination of neighboring towns of Ballwin and Manchester.

(21m) MANCHESTER. (Pop. 6,191). Originally called Hoardstown (after Jesse Hoard), it was changed in 1824 to Manchester by a local landowner from Manchester, England. Others say it was named for a settler who had been in the area as early as 1795, "old Mr. Manchester."
Springs Bar & Grill (L)(14424 Manchester), once the Tourist Hotel **(P44)**. City Hall is in the Lyceum (R)(14318). Built in 1894, it originally housed a tin shop and mercantile downstairs, and an auditorium upstairs. (On the National Register of Historic Places.)
Jct. MO 141 (Woods Mill Rd).

(23.5m) DES PERES. (Pop. 8,388). **Named for the River Des Peres ("de-pair," from the French for "of the Fathers"). The area has had a post office since 1848.**
Cross over I-270. Village Bar (L)(12247) next to the Diem House **(P43)**. 2 miles further to Kirkwood Rd.

Jct. Manchester Road & Kirkwood Rd (Lindbergh).

EITHER: Right on Kirkwood Rd (BYPASS 66) *(Recommended Route)*

KIRKWOOD. (Pop. 27,291). **This was the first planned residential community west of the Mississippi River. Originally called Dry Ridge, then Collins Station, in 1852 the newly organized town was renamed for James Pugh Kirkwood, chief engineer of the Pacific Railroad, who had laid out the route to the area being sold by land developers.**
Missouri Pacific Depot (R) **(P23)**. Spencer's Grill (R)(223 Kirkwood) **(P22)**. The Magic House (L)(516), a children's museum housed in a mansion built (1901) by the A.G. Edwards brokerage family. Proceed under I-44 to Watson Road. Westward Motel (L) **(P21)**. Jct. Watson & Kirkwood. Left (east) on Watson toward St. Louis. (See City 66 - Jct. Watson Road & US 67 - Kirkwood Rd - page 248.),

OR: Continue east on Manchester Road through **GLENDALE** (Pop. 5,945) to **ROCK HILL** (Pop. 5,217). Trainwreck Saloon (L)(9243 Manchester), originally the 9-Mile House **(P42)**. Follow Manchester through **BRENTWOOD** (Pop. 8,150) and **MAPLEWOOD** (Pop. 9,962) 6 miles to Jct. Manchester Rd & Vandeventer Ave. Left on Vandeventer 1/2 mile (2 stop lights) to Forest Park Pkwy.

[*NOTE: You pass Market St (R) (Old 66) that was cut off by US 40 (1937) as it entered downtown.*]

Right on Forest Park 1 mile to Market (Old 66). Continue east on Market. Union Station (R) **(P41)**. Kiel Center (R), originally called Municipal Auditorium **(P40)**. Jct. Market & Tucker (12th Street). City Hall (R) **(P5)**. Across Tucker is the Civil Courts building (L) **(P4)**. Left on Tucker, past the Jefferson Hotel (L)(415 Tucker) **(P3)**. Follow Tucker through the "S" curves into N. Florissant, veer left onto Palm (Natural Bridge) 2 blocks to Salisbury. Right, to McKinley Bridge **(P2)**, and over the Mississippi River into Illinois.

2) CITY 66.

[*NOTE: This became the main route in 1933.*]

Jct. MO 100 & I-44.
Odometer Notation: (0.0m)

From Gray Summit, proceed straight on I-44 south outer road.

m) PACIFIC. (Pop. 4,350). **The Pacific Railroad Company laid out the town in 1852 on** eir way to the Pacific Ocean. **Called Franklin, another name had to be taken for the new post** fice in 1854. **The building of the railroad had been stalled here for a couple of years (some** oney problems), so residents renamed the town for the railroad's hoped-for destination.

traight on Business Loop 44. Bridge (1932) over a deep cut for the Missouri Pacific acks that tunnel *under* the town of Gray Summit. The old Trails End Motel (R) •39). Across from the "caves" is a used car lot (R) that was the Cave Cafe **(P38).** ontinue through town past more caves (L), created by the mining of silica in the ndstone bluffs **(P37)**. Jensen Point (L) **(P36)**. Red Cedar Inn (L) **(P35)**. Cross bridge 1932) Fox Creek. Remains of the old Beacon Court (L) **(P34)** and the Al-Pac (L) **(P32,** 33).

3m) EUREKA. (Pop. 4,683). **In 1853 a surveying engineer for the railroad discovered that** route through this valley would eliminate many cuts and grades, and called the construction mp "Eureka" (Greek, meaning "I have found it!"). **ALLENTON** (R). **Named for Senator** homas R. Allen, president of the Pacific Railroad Company, who had laid out the town in 1852. he Henry Shaw Gardenway School Bus Stop (R) (c.1939).

NOTE: Old 66 serves as the I-44 on-ramp, then is under the interstate for the next 16 miles, except s noted.]

ast on I-44.

NOTE: Old 66 swung to the left of I-44 at **(12m)**,, *through Times Beach, over the old Meramec* iver bridge (1931) and past Steiny's Inn **(P31)**, *crossing back under the interstate.*]

12.5m) TIMES BEACH (L) (Pop. 0). **Times Beach was created to be a summer resort on** he Meramec River as a promotional gimmick by the St. Louis *Star-Times* in 1925. **The** ewspaper gave away 6-month subscriptions to all who bought a parcel lot, and held contests to ive away other lots. **In 1972-73, its dusty streets were sprayed with waste oil. In 1982 the town** eceived global notoriety when the Environmental Protection Agency disclosed that the oil ontained dioxin, and that the entire town was contaminated. By 1986 a government buyout was omplete, and Times Beach ceased to exist.

ross the Meramec River (a tribal word for "catfish"). Views of 66 **(P29, P30)**. **(19m)** ust prior to the start of the concrete wall median of I-44 is the site (R) of the old rav-O-Tel Deluxe Court **(P28)**.Valley Mount Ranch (R), offering horseback riding ince 1936.

'ENTON. (Pop. 3,346). **A post office since 1833, founder William Lindsay Long named the** own for his Welsh grandmother, Elizabeth Fenton Bennett.

Maritz Inc building (R), on the site of Dudley's Cabins and Service **(P27)**. 1/2 mile on he (R) is what's left of the Siesta Motel, next to the Rose Lawn Motel. Cross the Meramec River again. On the eastern bank was the old Sylvan Beach Park (L) **(P26)**.

Joplin to St. Louis

Continue on I-44 to Watson Road (Exit 277A). Straight. On the (L) is a Holiday Inn on the site of the Park Plaza Court (P25) and the Viking Conference Center, once Nelson's Cafe (P24). Jct. US 67 (Kirkwood Rd) cloverleaf (P20).

City 66 - Jct. Watson Road & US 67 (Kirkwood Rd).
(To bypass St. Louis, turn left on Kirkwood Rd. and follow BYPASS 66, page 249.)

CRESTWOOD. (Pop. 11,229). East on Watson Road (MO 366 - City 66). Lo (R)(10230 Watson) next to Color Art that was the site of Twin-Six Auto Court (P19) Johnny Mac's Sporting Goods (R)(10100), site of the Blue Bonnet Court (P18) Crestwood Medical Center (R)(10000), on the site of the Blue Haven Auto Cour (P17). National Food Center (R), on the site of the "66" Park In Theatre. (Operating continuously since 1946 to 1994, the theatre once offered such pre-movie extras a free pony rides, a Ferris wheel, slides, merry-go-round, and even a pair of trained bea cubs!) Roosevelt Bank (L)(9285), site of The Oaks Motel (P16). Across the road i Gundaker Realtors (R)(9282), the site where Motel Royal (P15) was located. Watso Plaza Auto Court (R)(8730), where 66 Auto Court (P14) was.

MARLBOROUGH. La Casa Grande Court (R)(8208) (c.1940) "Like A Fine Hotel. The Duplex Motel (R)(7898) (P13). Chippewa Motel (R)(7880) (P12). Wayside Cour (R)(7800) (P11). The old Coral Court Motel (L)(7755) (P10).

SHREWSBURY. (Pop. 6,416). **Platted in 1889, the town was named for a hamlet i England.**
Continue on Watson Road under the old wooden Frisco railroad trestle (1931).
St. Louis City Limit - Watson Rd becomes Chippewa (Algonquian for "puckered, referring to a moccasin style with puckered seams). Cross River Des Peres ("de-pair, from the French for "of the Fathers"). Ted Drewes Frozen Custard (R)(6726) (P9) Garavelli's Restaurant (R)(6600), once the Shangri-La (P8). Keller Pharmacy & Dru Store (L)(5201) (1934). Continue under the MoPac railroad overpass (1940) with it U-turn ramps above and pedestrian walkway below. Jct. Gravois (French for "gravel" Ave (1st light). Angle left onto Gravois for 3 miles, past Arrow Motors (L)(3185), o the site of Edmond's Restaurant (P97), and St. Francis De Sales Church (L) (P6). Vee left onto Tucker (12th Street) to Chouteau Av. Checkerboard Square - Ralston Purin world headquarters (R).

[*NOTE: The Municipal Bridge (P1), an alternate 66 route over the Mississippi River, is to the righ at Chouteau.*]

Jct. Market St. City Hall (L) (P5). Civil Courts building (R) (P4). Straight on Tucke by the Jefferson Hotel (L)(415) (P3), and through the "S" curves onto N. Florissan veer left onto Palm (Natural Bridge) 2 blocks to Salisbury. Right, to McKinley Bridg (P2), and over the Mississippi River into Illinois.

3) BYPASS 66.

Jct. MO 100 & I-44.
From Gray Summit,
EITHER: Follow ORIGINAL CITY 66 (page 244) to Jct. Manchester Road & Kirkwood (below) (27-1/2 miles),

OR: Follow CITY 66 (page 246) to Jct. Watson Road & US 67 (Kirkwood Rd) (25 miles). Left on Kirkwood Rd.

KIRKWOOD. (Pop. 27,291). **This was the first planned residential community west of the Mississippi River. Originally called Dry Ridge, then Collins Station, in 1852 the newly organized town was renamed for James Pugh Kirkwood, chief engineer of the Pacific Railroad, who had laid out the route to the area being sold by land developers.**
Westward Motel (R) **(P21)**. Follow Kirkwood Rd, passing The Magic House (R)(516 Kirkwood), a children's museum housed in a mansion built (1901) by the A.G. Edwards brokerage family, Spenser's Grill (L)(223) **(P22)**, and the Missouri Pacific Depot (L) **(P23)**. Continue on Kirkwood to Jct. Manchester Road.

Jct. Manchester Road & Kirkwood.
North on Lindbergh Rd (Kirkwood) (BYPASS 66) 13-1/2 miles to I-270.

[*NOTE: This bypass was established in the early 1930s and designated Route 66 in 1936.*]

FRONTENAC. (Pop. 3,411). **Named to honor the 17th century governor of Quebec, Louis de Baude, Comte De Palluau et De Frontenac (Count Frontenac).**
Frontenac Hilton (L)(1335), on the site of the old King Bros. Motel **(P61)**. Continue under new US 40 (I-64).

CREVE COEUR. (Pop. 12,889). **French for "broken heart," locals say the town received its name from the legend of an Indian maiden who was "heart-broken" because her love, a French trapper, never returned. She is said to have cried tears to form a lake in the shape of a broken heart, then drowned herself in its waters.**
World Headquarters for Monsanto (R-L).

MARYLAND HEIGHTS. (Pop. 25,407). **A post office since 1925, a local doctor from Maryland named his estate high on a hill "Maryland Heights."**

BRIDGETON. (Pop. 17,779). **Called Cottonwood Swamp, it was renamed Bridgeton in the early 1840s because one had to cross a stone bridge to reach town from either direction.**
Northwest Plaza entrance (R)(3700 block), site of the old Sunset Acres Motel **(P60)**. Cross over St. Charles Rock Rd (old US 40). Air-Way Motel (L)(4125), once Air-O-Way Courts **(P59)**. Cross over I-70. Stanley Cour-Tel (L)(4675) **(P58)**. Continue over Natural Bridge Road. Site (R) of Lambert Air Field **(P57)**.

(13m) HAZELWOOD. (Pop. 15,512). **Probably named after Hazelwood Farms. Senator Henry Clay of Kentucky, on a visit here in 1828, proclaimed a local orchard reminded him of his estate "Hazelwood." The owner renamed his farm, and the area followed suit.**
Aerial view of 66 **(P55)**. Airport Motel (L)(6221) **(P56)**. Jct. I-270. East on I-270 (1961).

[*NOTE: BYPASS 66 is under the interstate for the next 9-1/2 miles to Riverview Drive, the last Missouri exit.*]

(14m) FLORISSANT. (Pop. 51,208). **"Missouri French" for "fleurissant," meaning flowering, prosperous, or flourishing.**
John B. Myers House & Barn (L) **(P54)**.

(19m) BELLEFONTAINE NEIGHBORS. (Pop. 10,922). **Derived from the French "belle fontaine" (beautiful spring). Fort Bellefontaine (1805) was the first fort west of the Mississippi River.**

[*NOTE: Originally you left Missouri (on BYPASS 66) over the old Chain of Rocks Bridge* **(P52, P53)**.]

[To view the bridge, leave I-270 at Exit 34 (Riverview Drive) to the right. Close to the Missouri shore is the "Fortress," Intake Tower No. 1 (1894), used to draw water into St. Louis' system (crew quarters are above). Intake Tower No. 2 (1915) is closer to the old bridge.]

Rejoin I-270 East, crossing the Mississippi River on the new Chain of Rocks Bridge into Illinois.

SPECIAL THANKS

The author thanks all who contributed to this project, from you who provided photos from your family albums and postcards from your collections (Photo Credits), to those who helped determine historical data. This book would not have been possible without your eager assistance.

Special thanks to the following:
Wayne & Pat Bales (Route 66 Motors), Rolla; **Harrell Barber**, St. Clair; **Brad Beck** (Joplin Historical Society), Joplin; **Robert Bowers**, Springfield; **John Bradbury** (Western Historical Manuscript Collection), Rolla; **Hillary & Mary Brightwell**, Springfield; **Red & Julia Chaney**, Springfield; **Bruce & Thelma Debo** (Roubidoux Woodworkers), Devils Elbow; **Jonathan Delano** (Delano Oil Co.), St. James; **Emma Dunn**, Bourbon; **Fran Eickhoff** (Route 66 Lounge), Cuba; **Gary Ellison**, Springfield; **Jim Evans** (St. Clair Historical Society), St. Clair; **Larry Hager** (MO Highway & Transportation Dep't), Jefferson City; **Michael Glenn** (Springfield-Greene County Library), Springfield; **Elva Lee Henson** (Wayside Inn), Hazelgreen; **Tim & Alice Jones** (Totem Pole Trading Post), Rolla; **Ada Moore** (Hall-Moore Stuff Co.), Lebanon; **Kirk Pearce** (Lebanon Daily Record), Lebanon; **Jim Powell** (Missouri Route 66 Association), St. Louis; **Jack Roberts** (St. Clair Historical Society), St. Clair; **Venita Roberts**, Clementine; **Scott Sargent**, Lee's Summit; **Leo Scott** (Scott Welding), Sullivan; **Alf Smith**, Marshfield; **Vern Smith**, Buckhorn; the late **Vernon Starks**, St. Clair; **Mark Stauter** (Western Historical Manuscript Collection), Rolla; **Mary Lou Stone** (Richard's Antiques), Halltown; **Art & Bernie Whitworth**, Bourbon; **Karl & Esther Wickstrom**, Marshfield; and, of course, **Karla**.

PHOTO CREDITS

1 - 6: Postcards author's collection. **7:** Postcard Jim Powell collection, St. Louis. **8:** Postcard Alf D. Smith collection, Marshfield. **9:** Photo courtesy Ted Drewes, St. Louis. **10 - 11:** Postcards Wayne & Pat Bales collection, Rolla. **12:** Postcard Alf D. Smith collection, Marshfield. **13 - 15:** Postcards Scott Sargent collection, Lee's Summit. **16:** Postcard Jim Powell collection, St. Louis. **17:** Postcard author's collection. **18 - 19:** Postcards Wayne & Pat Bales collection, Rolla. **20:** Photo Massie Collection, Missouri State Archives, Jefferson City. **21:** Postcard Scott Sargent collection, Lee's Summit. **22:** Photo courtesy Mike Katsoulis, Kirkwood. **23:** Author's photo. **24:** Photo Massie Collection, Missouri State Archives, Jefferson City. **25:** Postcard Ada Moore collection, Lebanon. **26:** Postcard Scott Sargent collection, Lee's Summit. **27 - 28:** Postcards Jim Powell collection, St. Louis. **29 - 30:** Photos Missouri Highway Department, Jefferson City. **31:** Postcard Jim Powell collection, St. Louis. **32:** Photo author's collection. **33:** Postcard Wayne & Pat Bales collection, Rolla **34:** St. Clair Historical Society. **35 - 36:** Postcards Jim Powell collection., St. Louis. **37:** Author's photo. **38:** Postcard Scott Sargent collection, Lee's Summit. **39:** Photo courtesy Willard & Bernice Haley, Gray Summit. **40 - 41:** Postcards author's collection **42:** Photo courtesy George Hansford, St. Louis. **43:** Photo courtesy Pep Tomafovic, St. Louis. **44:** Photo courtesy Robert H. Ruck, Manchester. **45:** Western Historical Manuscript Collection-Rolla. **46:** Author's photo. **47:** Postcard author's collection. **48:** Photo courtesy Todd DeVille, St. Louis. **49:** Photo courtesy Claude Kelpe. **50:** Photo courtesy Doris Bryan, St. Clair. **51:** Photo courtesy Janet Daniel, Gray Summit. **52:** Postcard Ada Moore collection, Lebanon. **53:** Postcard Scott Sargent collection, Lee's Summit. **54:** Photo courtesy Rosemary Davidson, Florissant. **55:** Photo courtesy Hazelwood City Hall. **56:** Photo courtesy Carl & Rose DeGrasso, Hazelwood. **57:** Postcard Alf D. Smith collection, Marshfield. **58 - 60:** Postcards Jim Powell collection, St. Louis. **61:** Postcard Wayne & Pat Bales collection, Rolla. **62:** Photo courtesy Janet Daniel, Gray Summit. **63:** St. Clair Historical Society. **64:** Postcard Jim Powell collection, St. Louis. **65:** Photo courtesy Evelyne Ruth Meyer, Pacific. **66:** Postcard Jim Powell collection, St. Louis. **67:** Postcard Scott Sargent collection, Lee's Summit. **68:** Postcard courtesy Mary & Jim Ming, Villa Ridge. **69:** St. Clair Historical Society. **70:** Postcard Wayne & Pat Bales collection, Rolla. **71:** Photo courtesy Max & Laverta Pracht, Union. **72:** St. Clair Historical Society. **73:** Postcard Scott Sargent collection, Lee's Summit. **74 - 77:** St. Clair Historical Society. **78:** Photo courtesy Almond & Mildred Dall, Sullivan. **79 - 80:** Photos courtesy Jerome & Danny Ritter, St. Clair. **81:** Postcard author's collection. **82 - 86:** St. Clair Historical Society. **87:** Postcard Scott Sargent collection, Lee's Summit. **88:** Postcard Wayne & Pat Bales collection, Rolla. **89:** Postcard John F. Bradbury Jr. collection, Rolla. **90:** Photo courtesy Ralph Jones, Rolla. **91:** St. Clair Historical Society. **92:** Postcard Wayne & Pat Bales collection, Rolla. **93:** Photo courtesy Dave & Jan Wall, Stanton. **94:** Postcard Jim Powell collection, St. Louis. **95:** Postcard Wayne & Pat Bales collection, Rolla. **96:** Postcard Jim Powell collection, St. Louis. **97:** Postcard Scott Sargent collection, Lee's Summit. **98 - 99:** Photos courtesy William & Agnes Juergens, Sullivan. **100:** Postcard Scott Sargent collection, Lee's Summit. **101:** Photo courtesy Emma Dunn, Bourbon. **102:** Photo courtesy Kermit & Faye Roedemeier, Bourbon. **103:** Author's photo. **104:** Photo courtesy Marge Davis, Bourbon. **105 - 106:** Photos courtesy Art & Bernie Whitworth, Bourbon. **107:** Photo courtesy Alfreda & Anthony Cios, Bourbon. **108:** Photo courtesy Marea Land, Bourbon. **109:** Postcard courtesy Deborah Warning Ransom, Springfield. **110:** Photo courtesy Marvin & Kathryn Libhart, Cuba. **111:** Photo courtesy Emma Dunn, Bourbon. **112 - 113:** Photo & postcard courtesy Kenny Killeen, Cuba. **114:** Postcard Wayne & Pat Bales collection, Rolla. **115:** Postcard courtesy Cordell Perkins, Cuba. **116:** Photo courtesy Wilbur Vaughn, Cuba. **117 - 118:** Photos courtesy James Barnett Jr., Cuba. **119:** Postcard author's collection. **120:** Author's photo. **121 - 122:** Photos courtesy James Memorial Library, St. James. **123:** Photo courtesy Jonathan Delano, St. James. **124:** Photo courtesy John Bullock, St. James. **125 - 126:** Photos courtesy Ruth Waring, St. James. **127:** Postcard courtesy Josephine Nowak, St. James. **128:** Photo courtesy Wayne & Pat Bales, Rolla. **129:** Postcard author's collection. **130:** Postcard Wayne & Pat Bales collection, Rolla. **131:** Photo Missouri Highway Department, Jefferson City. **132:** Postcard John F. Bradbury Jr. collection, Rolla. **133:** Postcard Wayne & Pat Bales collection, Rolla. **134 - 135:** Postcards John F. Bradbury Jr. collection, Rolla. **136:** Photo courtesy George Carney, Rolla. **137 - 138:** Postcards Alf D. Smith collection, Marshfield. **139 - 142:** Postcards John F. Bradbury Jr. collection, Rolla. **143:** Photo courtesy Virginia Martin, Martin Spring. **144:** Photo courtesy Bill Aaron Sr., Rolla. **145:** Photo Western Historical Manuscript Collection-Rolla. **146:** Photo courtesy Tim & Alice Jones, Rolla. **147:** Photo courtesy of Dan Malone, Doolittle. **148:** Photo courtesy Kirk Pearce, Lebanon. **149:** Postcard John F. Bradbury Jr. collection, Rolla. **150 - 151:** Photos Western Historical Manuscript Collection-Rolla. **152:** Postcard author's collection. **153:** Photo courtesy Ralph Jones, Rolla. **154 - 155:** Photos courtesy Tim & Alice Jones, Rolla. **156:** Postcard Scott Sargent collection, Lee's Summit. **157:** Photo courtesy George Carney, Rolla. **158:** Photo Missouri Highway Department, Jefferson City. **159:** Postcard John F. Bradbury Jr. collection, Rolla. **160:** Photo courtesy Earl E. Nicks, Richland. **161:** Postcard John F. Bradbury Jr. collection, Rolla. **162:** Photo courtesy Venita Roberts, Newburg. **163:** Postcard courtesy Sterling Wells, St. Robert. **164:** Author's photo. **165:** Postcard courtesy Norman Stoll, Richland. **166:** Photo Massie Collection, Missouri State Archives, Jefferson City. **167:** Postcard Ada Moore collection, Lebanon. **168:** Photo Missouri Highway Department, Jefferson City. **169:** Postcard Wayne & Pat Bales collection, Rolla. **170:** Photo courtesy Larry & Eula West, St. Robert. **171 - 172:** Postcards John F. Bradbury Jr. collection, Rolla. **173:** Postcard courtesy Steve Beattie, Waynesville. **174 - 175:** Postcards Alf D. Smith collection, Marshfield.

176 - 177: Postcard & photo courtesy Atholl (Jiggs) & Dorothy Miller, Devils Elbow. 178: Photo courtesy Jane Graham King, Waynesville. 179: Author's photo. 180: Postcard Scott Sargent collection, Lee's Summit. 181: Author's photo. 182: Photo courtesy Steve Beattie, Waynesville. 183: Postcard Alf D. Smith collection, Marshfield. 184 - 186: Postcards John F. Bradbury Jr. collection, Rolla. 187: Postcard Alf D. Smith collection, Marshfield. 188 - 189: Photos courtesy of Don Deutschman, Buckhorn. 190: Photo courtesy Norman Stoll, Richland. 191 - 192: Photos courtesy Vern Smith, Buckhorn. 193: Postcard courtesy Earl E. Nicks, Richland. 194: Photo courtesy Leroy Roberson, Richland. 195: Postcard John F. Bradbury Jr. collection, Rolla. 196: Photo courtesy Leroy Roberson, Richland. 197: Photo courtesy Norman Stoll, Richland. 198: Postcard Ada Moore collection, Lebanon. 199: Photo Kirk Pearce collection, Lebanon. 200 - 201: Photos courtesy Bonnie Watkins Middleswart & Joan Lee Watkins Cornelison, Lebanon. 202: Postcard John F. Bradbury Jr. collection, Rolla. 203: Photo courtesy Herschel Moore, Richland. 204: Postcard Scott Sargent collection, Lee's Summit. 205: Photo courtesy Judy Lorance French, Lebanon. 206: Photo Kirk Pearce collection, Lebanon. 207 - 208: Postcard & photo courtesy Ruth Riley, Wallops Island, VA. 209 - 210: Postcards Ada Moore collection, Lebanon. 211: Postcard Scott Sargent collection, Lee's Summit. 212: Postcard Ada Moore collection, Lebanon. 213: Postcard John F. Bradbury Jr. collection, Rolla. 214: Postcard courtesy Ramona Lehman, Lebanon. 215: Key courtesy Clyde Lorance, Springfield. 216 - 217: Postcard & photo Ada Moore collection, Lebanon. 218: Photo Massie Collection, Missouri State Archives, Jefferson City. 219 - 220: Photos courtesy Joy Spears Fishel, Springfield. 221 - 222: Postcards Kirk Pearce collection, Lebanon. 223: Photo courtesy Ron & Martha Young, Ozark. 224: Postcard author's collection. 225: Photo courtesy Doris Knight Lafferty, Lebanon. 226: Photo courtesy H.P. Montgomery Jr., Springfield. 227 - 228: Photos courtesy Beth Owen, Lebanon. 229: Postcard Ada Moore collection, Lebanon. 230: Photo courtesy Ron & Martha Young, Ozark. 231: Photo courtesy Izola Henson, Lebanon. 232: Postcard courtesy Kirk Pearce, Lebanon. 233: Author's photo. 234 - 235: Photos courtesy Ron & Martha Young, Ozark. 236: Postcard Ada Moore collection, Lebanon. 237 - 239: Photos courtesy Marie Harris Kennamer, Conway. 240: Postcard Scott Sargent collection, Lee's Summit. 241: Photo courtesy Hermon & Cleta Pearce, Marshfield. 242: Photo courtesy Robert & Pat Abbott, Marshfield. 243 - 245: Photos & postcard courtesy Randy Clair, Marshfield. 246 - 247: Postcards courtesy Clyde Kensinger, Springfield. 248: Postcard Ada Moore collection, Lebanon. 249: Photo courtesy Jack McDowell, Springfield. 250: Postcard Scott Sargent collection, Lee's Summit. 251: Photo courtesy Bill Johnmeyer, Springfield. 252: Author's photo. 253: Postcard Kirk Pearce collection, Lebanon. 254: Postcard Jim Powell collection, St. Louis. 255: Postcard Wayne & Pat Bales collection, Rolla. 256: Postcard Jim Powell collection, St. Louis. 257: Postcard John F. Bradbury Jr. collection, Rolla. 258: Postcard Ada Moore collection, Lebanon. 259 - 260: Postcards Robert Bowers collection, Springfield. 261: Postcard Wayne & Pat Bales collection, Rolla. 262 - 263: Postcards courtesy Hillary & Mary Brightwell, Springfield. 264: Postcard Alf D. Smith collection, Marshfield. 265 - 266: Postcards Scott Sargent collection, Lee's Summit. 267 - 268: Photos courtesy Donna Elkins, Springfield. 269: Postcard author's collection. 270: Postcard Wayne & Pat Bales collection, Rolla. 271 - 272: Postcards Jim Powell collection, St. Louis. 273 - 274: Postcards Wayne & Pat Bales collection, Rolla. 275: Postcard Jim Powell collection, St. Louis. 276: Postcard John F. Bradbury Jr. collection, Rolla. 277 - 278: Postcards Scott Sargent collection, Lee's Summit. 279 - 280: Photos The History Museum for Springfield/Greene County. 281: Postcard Robert Bowers collection, Springfield. 282: Photo courtesy Carl Hamby, Springfield. 283: Postcard Shepard Room Collection, Springfield Greene Co. Library. 284: Photo courtesy Lora Rogers, Springfield. 285: Postcard The History Museum for Springfield/Greene County. 286: Postcard Wayne & Pat Bales collection, Rolla. 287: Postcard Alf D. Smith collection, Marshfield. 288: Photo Massie Collection, Missouri State Archives, Jefferson City. 289 - 290: Postcards Wayne & Pat Bales collection, Rolla. 291: Postcard author's collection. 292: Postcard John F. Bradbury Jr. collection, Rolla. 293: Photo The History Museum for Springfield/Greene County. 294 - 295: Postcards Wayne & Pat Bales collection, Rolla. 296: Postcard Eula Mae Curtis collection, Springfield. 297: Postcard Alf D. Smith collection, Marshfield. 298: Postcard Shepard Room - Springfield Greene Co. Library. 299: Postcard Robert Bowers collection, Springfield. 300: Postcard The History Museum for Springfield/Greene County. 301: Photo courtesy Si Simon, Springfield. 302 - 303: Postcards Eula Mae Curtis collection, Springfield. 304 - 305: Photos courtesy Springfield Landmarks Preservation Trust. 306: Postcard Eula Mae Curtis collection, Springfield. 307: Photo The History Museum for Springfield/Greene County. 308: Photo courtesy Jim Hawkins, Springfield. 309: Postcard Robert Bowers collection, Springfield. 310: Postcard Wayne & Pat Bales collection, Rolla. 311 - 312: Photos courtesy Julia & Sheldon (Red) Chaney, Springfield. 313: Postcard Jim Powell collection, St. Louis. 314: Photo The History Museum for Springfield/Greene County. 315: Postcard Eula Mae Curtis collection, Springfield. 316: Postcard courtesy Marie Farley, Springfield. 317: Postcard Alf D. Smith collection, Marshfield. 318: Postcard Jim Powell collection, St. Louis. 319: Postcard Wayne & Pat Bales collection, Rolla. 320 - 321: Photos courtesy Dan & Dolores Wiley, Springfield. 322 - 323: Photos courtesy Mrs. Clell (Ruth) Barnes, Springfield. 324: Postcard John F. Bradbury Jr. collection, Rolla. 325: Postcard Jim Powell collection, St. Louis. 326 - 327: Photos courtesy Mary Lou Stone, Halltown. 328: Postcard Scott Sargent collection, Lee's Summit. 329 - 330: Postcards Jim Powell collection, St. Louis. 331 - 332: Postcards Scott Sargent collection, Lee's Summit. 333: Postcard Alf D. Smith collection, Marshfield. 334: Postcard Scott Sargent collection, Lee's Summit. 335: Postcard Jim Powell collection, St. Louis. 336: Postcard Ada Moore collection, Lebanon. 337: Postcard Scott Sargent collection, Lee's Summit. 338 - 339: Postcards John F. Bradbury Jr. collection, Rolla. 340 - 341: Postcards Scott Sargent collection, Lee's Summit. 342: Postcard Wayne & Pat Bales collection, Rolla. 343: Postcard Scott Sargent collection, Lee's Summit. 344 - 346: Postcards John F. Bradbury Jr. collection, Rolla. 347: Postcard Ada Moore collection, Lebanon. 348 - 349: Postcards Alf D. Smith collection, Marshfield. 350: Postcard Scott Sargent collection, Lee's Summit. 351: Photo The History Museum for Springfield/Greene Co.

REFERENCE SOURCES

AAA Directory Motor Courts & Cottages. American Automobile Association. Washington, D.C., 1939.

AAA Directory of Accommodations. American Automobile Association. Washington, D.C., 1946.

Andre, R. Miriam. *The Moving Forces in the History of Old BonHomme-The Manchester, Missouri Area.* 1982.

Andrews, Wayne, ed. *Concise Dictionary of American History.* New York: Charles Scribner's Sons, 1962.

Angus, Fern. *Down The Wire Road In The Missouri Ozarks.* 1992.

Beard, Louis Roper. *History of Laclede County, Missouri.* 1979.

Bradbury, John F., Jr. "Route 66 East to West. A Self-Guided Tour Through Phelps County." *Newsletter of the Phelps County Historical Society.* April, 1994.

A Century Passes but Memory Lingers On. Sullivan Centennial Committee, 1960.

The City of Hazelwood. City of Hazelwood, Missouri, 1992.

Conoco Travel Bureau Hotel and Cottage Camp Directory. Continental Oil Co., 1935

Conoco Travel Bureau Touraide-North Central Section. Continental Oil Co., 1936.

Coyle, Elinor Martineau. *Saint Louis - Portrait of a River City.* St. Louis: Folkestone Press, 1966.

Crawford County, Mo. 1829-1987. Crawford Co. History Book Committee. Paducah, KY: Turner Publishing Co., 1987.

Curtis, C.H. (Skip). *Why'd They Name It That? A Look At Some "Peculiar" Missouri Towns.* Lake St. Louis: Curtis Enterprises, 1992.

Daub, Chylene Jahn. *Ellisville Missouri 1932-1982.* City of Ellisville, Missouri, 1983.

Dunn, Emma J. *Bourbon, Missouri - A Picture History of a Small Town.* 1988.

Fifield, Barringer. *Seeing Saint Louis.* St. Louis: Washington University, 1987.

Franklin Co., Mo. Sesquicentennial. Franklin Co. and Pacific, Mo. 150 Years Young. Pacific Chamber of Commerce, 1968.

George, Flay Watters. *History of Webster County.* 1955.

Gould's St. Louis City and County Directory, 1926 through 1955.

Grosenbaugh, Dick. *A Million Hours of Memories. A Condensed History of Springfield, Missouri.* 1979.

History of Laclede, Camden, Dallas, Webster, Wright, Texas, Pulaski, Phelps and Dent Counties, Missouri. Chicago: The Goodspeed Publishing Co., 1889.

History of Pulaski County, Missouri. Pulaski County Historical Society, 1982.

Lawrence County, Missouri. 1945-1970. Lawrence County Historical Society, 1970.

Livingston, Joel T. *History of Jasper County, Missouri and Its People.* 1912.

Mann, Dr. & Mrs. Clair V. *The Story of Rolla, Missouri.* Rolla Bicentennial Commission and the Rolla Area Chamber of Commerce, 1974.

Mottaz, Mabel Manes. *Lest We Forget - A History of Pulaski County, Missouri and Fort Leonard Wood.* 1960.

National Register of Historic Places. 1966-1991. Ass'n for State & Local History-Nashville, TN; Nat'l Park Service-Washington, D.C.; Nat'l Conference of State Historic Preservation. Washington, D.C., 1991.

1992 Service Ratings for Bridges. Missouri Highway & Transportation Dep't - Division of Planning, 1992.

Polk's St. Louis City and County Directory, 1926 through 1955.

Polk's Springfield City Directory, 1926 through 1965.

Project History Maps. Missouri Highway & Transportation Dep't - Division of Planning, Jefferson City.

Reed, Sue and Eloise LeSaulnier. *In Retrospect...A Bicentennial Review of our Historic Heritage.* Missouri Publ. Co., 1976.

Rittenhouse, Jack D. *A Guide Book to Highway 66* (a facsimile of the 1946 first edition). Albuquerque: Univ. of New Mexico Press, 1989.

Roadside America: The Automobile in Design and Culture, ed. Jan Jennings. Iowa St. Press, 1990.

Route 66 Collection. Western Historical Manuscript Collection-Rolla. Rolla, MO.

Schultz, Robert G. *Missouri Post Offices 1804-1981.* St. Louis: American Philatelic Society, 1982.

Scott, Quinta and Susan Croce Kelly. *Route 66: The Highway and Its People.* Norman: Univ. of Oklahoma Press, 1988.

Shell Tourist Accommodation Directory-North Central States. Shell Petroleum Co., 1938 and 1939.

Snyder, Tom. *The Route 66 Traveler's Guide and Roadside Companion.* New York: St. Martin's Press, 1990.

Spears-Stewart, Rita. *Remembering The Ozark Jubilee.* Stewart, Dillbeck & White Productions, 1993.

The State of Missouri, ed. Walter Williams. Louisana Purchase Exposition, 1904.

State of Missouri Book, ed. H.R. Walmsley. State of Missouri Book Trust, 1932.

Stolwyk, Carl F. and Florence G. *A History of Des Peres, Missouri.* City of Des Peres, Missouri, 1976.

Teague, Tom. *Searching For 66.* Springfield, IL: Samizdat House, 1991.

Wallace, Caverly Scott and Dorthea M. Loehr. *A History Of Ballwin Missouri.* The City of Ballwin, 1979.

Wallis, Michael. *Route 66: The Mother Road.* New York: St. Martin's Press, 1990.

Works Project Administration, Writers' Program. *Missouri, A Guide to the "Show Me" State.* New York: Duell, Sloan and Pearce, 1941.

INDEX

Why'd They Name It That?

Why'd They Name It That? (A Look At Some "Peculiar" Missouri Towns) is another book by Missourian C.H. (Skip) Curtis. Now, in what the Springfield *News-Leader* calls "...a fun volume of history and trivia," you can discover why anyone would name a town Jerktail...Rat...or Tightwad! You'll find out what was going on to call an area Peculiar. And learn what makes a place Useful!

A recent issue of the American Library Association's *Booklist* states "...Curtis does a nice job of seeking out those mostly small Missouri towns with odd or provocative names, finding a representative (full-page) photograph, and providing a history of the name." The *Missouri Historical Review* of The State Historical Society notes that "the excellent photographs and attractive design greatly enhance this entertaining volume."

The origins of over 160 place names of Missouri towns are examined, including Success, Rover, Blue Eye, Clever, Frankenstein and Ink.

A great gift idea!

Please send the following:
( ) **copy/copies of *Why'd They Name It That?* ($19.95 ea.)**   _____

SALES TAX: Add $1.44 per book   _____
            (for books shipped to a MO address)

SHIPPING & HANDLING: Add $2.00 per book   ══════

                                        TOTAL _____

_____
Name

_____
Address

_____
City   State   Zip Code

(I understand that I may return any books for a full refund)

Please make check payable to:
CURTIS ENTERPRISES
2302 Gascony Drive
Lake St. Louis, MO 63367
(314) 625-8267

THE

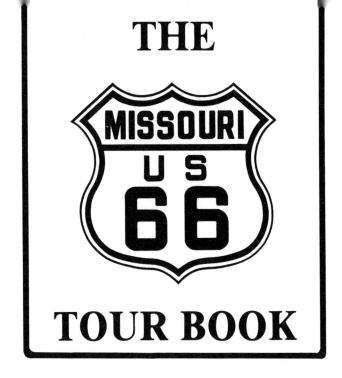

TOUR BOOK

ORDER FORM

(I understand that I may return any books for a full refund)

Please send the following:

( ) copy/copies of *The Missouri US 66 Tour Book* ($29.95 ea.) _____

SALES TAX: Add $2.16 per book _____
(for books shipped to a MO address)

SHIPPING & HANDLING: Add $2.00 per book _____

TOTAL _____

_____
Name

_____
Address

_____
City   State   Zip Code

Please make check payable to:
CURTIS ENTERPRISES
424 S. National
Springfield, MO 65802
417-866-4743